This book is dedicated to Katie, Selena and Keith, and all of the good and decent cops I was lucky enough to work with.

CHASING KILLERS

THREE DECADES OF CRACKING CRIME IN THE UK'S MURDER CAPITAL

JOE JACKSON

MAINSTREAM
PUBLISHING
EDINBURGH AND LONDON

First published in Great Britain in 2008 by
MAINSTREAM PUBLISHING COMPANY
(EDINBURGH) LTD
7 Albany Street
Edinburgh EH1 3UG

ISBN 9781845964061

A catalogue record for this book is available
from the British Library

Typeset in Garamond and Trixie

Printed in Great Britain by
CPI Mackays Ltd, Chatham ME5 8TD

Acknowledgements

I have been goaded, cajoled and encouraged all the way by my wife Katie and daughter Selena. Through their determination, and with the tremendous help and skill of seasoned author Douglas Skelton, I have finally managed to put this book together. I also wish to thank Bill Campbell of Mainstream for taking a chance on me and to express my gratitude to the pictorial staff of the *Daily Record*, to the editorial staff of the *Scottish Daily Express* and to my trusted friend, the well-known *Sunday Mail* journalist Norman Silvester.

Contents

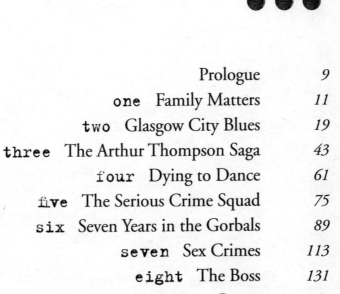

Prologue

30 November 1976

It was a nightmarish journey in more ways than one.

The raging blizzard threw itself at the car windows as I headed south down the icy A74. Inside, nothing much was said between me and my three colleagues. There wasn't much that could be said. The soft scrape of the wipers sweeping the snow away from the windscreen was, for long periods, the only sound in the car. But no matter how much they cleared, there was always more ready to launch at us.

That snowstorm was a bit like my working life. For sixteen years, I had helped protect the public from the most evil people in Scotland but as soon as we rid the streets of one monster there was another ready to take his place. For sixteen years, I had been chasing crooks and killers and had used the law to put them away. Now, I was chasing two of the worst villains I'd ever encountered and I was more than ready to use the gun under my coat to put them down. They had escaped from the most secure mental facility in Scotland, brutally killing a nurse, another patient and a police officer. They were on the run.

There was no way in hell there would be any more innocent victims of their madness. When we caught up with them, if either of these men so much as pointed a finger at us they would be in my line of fire. There would be no ifs, no buts, no second thoughts. Their guilt was not in doubt.

I am sure that my three stony-faced colleagues were of the same mind. We had not discussed it. The resolve was something unsaid, a fifth passenger in that car heading southwards.

Sixteen years of chasing killers.

Sixteen years of pursuing the evidence, building the case, following the rules.

Now, I was prepared to shoot to kill in order to bring to a halt this particular trail of terror and blood and death. I would do what was needed, even if that meant delivering summary justice.

Sixteen years on the job. When I joined the force, I would never have believed that it would come to this. And I didn't know on that dark night if there would be another sixteen years . . .

Family Matters

I wish I could say I always wanted to be a cop but that wasn't the case. I wanted to be a cowboy. Unfortunately, there wasn't much scope for herding cattle in Glasgow. Later, a love of words made me yearn to be a journalist. Policing may have been in my future but it was not in my blood and it did not register on my youthful radar.

My father, known as Big Joe despite being only 5 ft 9 in., had two younger brothers, John and James. Their father was a carter whose job took him into the distilleries and breweries dotted throughout Glasgow and he invariably returned from deliveries with his horse's feed pail full of booze – in fact, he had a conviction for being drunk in charge of his horse and cart. He was certainly in the habit of 'taking a good bucket'. I think his horse was teetotal, though.

My grandfather smoked a clay pipe and had a spittoon in his living room, which he could hit from 20 paces. In 1892, the Buffalo Bill Wild West Show came to Glasgow and as a young boy he had been hired to help look after the horses. It was the only thing that impressed me about him.

My father worked as a foreman in the Stewart and Lloyd's steel plant in Bridgeton. His job was classified as necessary for the war effort, so he was exempt from call-up during the Second World War. A very fit man, he was a First Division football referee until the age of 52 and officiated at many Cup finals, internationals and Old Firm encounters. His normal payment for a First Division game was £5 plus expenses but for Cup finals or internationals he received the princely sum of £10. One of his claims to fame was that he sent off the famous Rangers and international centre-half, Willie Woodburn, when Rangers were playing against Clyde. As a result of this, when I turned up for my first day at secondary school, there was a posse waiting for me and I received a severe bleaching. I went home at lunchtime with my new blazer in tatters and got a cuff round the ear from my mum. Talk about the sins of the fathers . . .

My dad didn't realise how funny he could be, because he was so carried away with his own importance. He occasionally partook of a few shandies after a game and then he could be a great source of hilarity to the rest of the family. The proud owner of a pair of false teeth, he once forgot to take them out before being sick down the toilet and accidentally flushed them down the pan. Another time, not feeling too bright after a night on the tiles, he stuck his head out of his bedroom window to cough and fired his false teeth out onto the path below. They didn't survive the fall. It cost him three weeks' wages to get another pair hurriedly made for the next match, an Old Firm Cup final. He discovered that he had problems holding his whistle with his new gnashers, so he conducted the game with a series of hand signals. It's a pity referees weren't sponsored in those days – he would have been a prime candidate for the local dentist.

After he retired as a referee, he never went to games as a spectator – with one exception. In the run-up to the 1967 European Cup final, a Scottish newspaper ran a competition with the prize of a trip to

Lisbon to see the match. Surprisingly, my dad decided to enter. He submitted a description of an incident in a match he had refereed, in which there had been a hard clash between a Celtic player and one of the opposing team. Footballers were made of stern stuff in those days and after the collision the two players got up, dusted themselves down and continued to play. The Celtic player completed the 90 minutes and came off the field before complaining of a pain in his leg. It turned out he had sustained a fracture to his tibia.

This piece of football reportage actually won the competition and Dad went to Lisbon to witness the famous victory by Celtic Football Club over Inter Milan – the one and only time he ever travelled abroad. When he came home, my brothers and I asked him avidly all about the match but it would appear that he had imbibed too much of the local wine and was not clear as to what he had actually witnessed. Considerately, he had brought my mother a present. This consisted of the pre-packed meal he had received on the plane on the homeward journey!

My mother, Janet, was one of a family of fifteen children. Her father, a blacksmith of Irish descent, was by all accounts a large, strong man who became known as Big Daddy. During service in the First World War as a soldier in the artillery, he was gassed and never fully recovered his health. He died at the beginning of the Second World War. My maternal grandmother was a Tennant, probably from Lanarkshire. I remember her as a lovely old woman who never got over the death of her husband. She became senile early and every day she used to walk the two miles from her home on the outskirts of Tollcross to the shops, often coming back laden, even though her family were all married and had left home many years before. In her kitchen, she had a big stone washing boiler that was full of unused potatoes.

My mother and father met in the late 1920s. She was a weaver in the Templeton Carpet Factory in Bridgeton. The factory is gone now but the building remains, a red-brick, castellated structure on the fringes of Glasgow Green. After their wedding, she gave up work in order to be a housewife, which was usual for women in those days. She raised four children, Jim, Betty, John and me. We lived in a tenement in Springfield Road in the heart of Bridgeton. Our house consisted of a kitchen, a small hallway and a bedroom. My parents had a double bed in a recess in the kitchen, which I sometimes shared with my mother when my father was working night shifts. I was born in 1940, in the days before the inception of the National Health Service, so no doctor was called when my mother was giving birth. Doctors were too expensive. A midwife was paid five shillings for delivering me – my father later said it was the worst five shillings he had ever spent. All the kids shared one room, the three boys sleeping in a double bed, my sister enjoying the luxury of a single bed. Billy Connolly's joke regarding the duvet cover having sleeves was literally true, as the covers consisted of ex-army blankets and second-hand coats. There was no central heating in the house but that didn't matter because there was no electricity either. There were gas mantles for lighting and the main form of cooking was on a big black-leaded range, which provided heat and hot water. Carpets were unheard of in working-class homes.

The toilet – and it was just a toilet, with no basin or bath – was on the landing; we shared it with two other families on the same floor. Newspapers were multi-functional. After you read them, they were cut into squares and stuck on a nail in the toilet. There was gas lighting in the close and the gas lamps out on the street were lit by lamplighters – they always seemed to be small men – who were supplied with ladders to reach the lamps. I always thought that the council could have saved a fortune on ladders if they had employed taller lamplighters.

There was a war on, so it was very difficult for anyone to get proper rations or luxury items, even if they could afford them. At the end of the war, when supplies were reaching us from America, I remember sharing with the rest of the family the first tinned fruit we had ever seen – a can of fruit cocktail. This was kept as a special treat for Sunday dinner – only posh folk had lunch. I managed to snaffle the only bright-red cherry in the dish.

Some nights, the Germans attempted to bomb a nearby power station and all the families in our close had to get to the bottom floor, which was reinforced with wooden beams. My brother John would somehow contrive to sleep soundly throughout these bombardments.

I was, I suppose, a typical street urchin. When I was about four or five, I had the good luck while playing to be struck on the head by a large, metal Capstan cigarette sign, which fell from its perch outside a sweetie shop. My mother carried me down to the main junction at Dalmarnock Road, where there was a policeman on points duty. He immediately stopped a coal lorry and instructed the driver to take us to the Royal Infirmary. Even though I was bleeding profusely, I thoroughly enjoyed my first trip in a motorised vehicle. That, however, was not the good luck – I was wearing my grandfather's forage cap from the First World War, which protected my young head, and although I sustained a wound that required six stitches, it could have been much worse. Sweets were rationed during the war but after my 'misfortune' the shopkeeper was always lenient with me if I did not have sufficient coupons.

On another occasion, I was run over by a tramcar while crossing the street. The driver dropped the 'cow-catcher' at the front of the vehicle, which scooped me up, saving me from serious injury. This episode unfortunately led to more head damage but not more sweets!

I went to Springfield Road Primary School at five years of age. John was still at this school and was known as a good fighter. I did not aspire to his title but on occasion was forced to uphold the Jackson name and became embroiled in scraps. The fact that I was a natural left-hander did not sit well with the teaching staff. They usually said that it made the class look awkward or untidy if I wrote with my left hand and attempted to remedy this by tying the sleeve of my jumper over the offending hand, causing me to look like Quasimodo. How this tidied up the class I don't know, but it had the desired effect in that I became totally proficient with my right hand and was also able to write with the other. I attended diligently to all my classwork and as a result I was the recipient of annual prizes throughout my time at primary school.

When I was eight, the family flitted to a new housing estate, Greenfield, where we moved into a semi-detached house. Coming from the cramped existence of the tenement, this was sheer luxury. We'd never had a bath in the house before and had grown used to washing at the kitchen sink and making the weekly pilgrimage to the public baths in Shettleston. The new house had an amazing three bedrooms upstairs: one for my parents, one for Betty and the biggest one for the three sons. Downstairs, there was an L-shaped sitting room and dining area and a kitchen. This was style.

I transferred to Shettleston Primary School, where I got my first chance to play for a school football team. I stuck in at my lessons there and when I moved on to secondary school I won the top prize for studies during my first term at Eastbank Academy. After this, my interest in scholarly pursuits waned considerably. I did, however, play for all of the school football teams, was in the gym team and swam for the school. I developed an interest in cycling and this took up most of my free time.

My father was a foreman labourer with no trade and he thought that if his sons became tradesmen, then they were doing all right. I left school at 15 years old and followed my brothers into the dirtiest trade of all, plastering. We all worked for a company called George Rome and Sons. My starting wage was a shilling (5p) an hour for working 44 hours a week over six days, with a half-day on Saturdays. One of my crowning achievements during my first year of employment was to work for 105 hours in one week to earn a total of 5 pounds 5 shillings. The taxman took 5 shillings, so I was able to take home a fiver and was delighted. It didn't matter to me that I had to work from 8 a.m. till 10 p.m. each day to achieve this.

My eldest brother, Jim, was a complex character who started to go bald when he was still in his teens, which deeply affected him, causing him to become moody and introverted. He kept telling me that I had the same type of hair and would also lose it at an early stage. This is not what a boy of 14 wants to hear. John was completely opposite in character to Jim. Confident in his charisma and looks, he was fairly wild and my mother took to searching his pockets after he had been out on the town. She found various things, ranging from contraceptives to knuckle-dusters. She tried some unusual ploys to dissuade him from his capers – once, when he arrived home from work and was seated with the rest of us at the dinner table, he was presented with a plate, not of cod and chips, but condoms and chibs.

I worked as a plasterer until I was 19 years old, still maintaining my interest in cycling but also attending the various dance halls in Glasgow. The Dennistoun Palais was a favourite, as was the Locarno in Sauchiehall Street. The Barrowland Ballroom was not quite as good, partly because the bouncers were tougher and there were not as many entertaining fights as at the Palais. In later years, I would return to the Barrowland as part of a team trying to track down a murderer. There were many dance halls in Glasgow at this time but I generally did not stray out of my own area. You were never well received where you were not known. I tried to steer clear of trouble. It was a hard environment and rather dangerous for a young, good-looking male. Luckily, I was quite safe.

The dirt and grime of four years of plastering proved to be enough. I was looking for something else, although I didn't know what. My brother John had joined the police force six months earlier. Jim had also tried but he was considered too old and in any case he was colour blind. Without any real sense of motivation, I followed their lead and decided to give it a shot.

Glasgow City Blues

My initial training at the Scottish Police College in Whitburn was completely engrossing and I soon realised how much I wanted to make a go of this profession. However, some of my fellow trainees were plainly chancers and experience was shortly to disabuse me of my innocent belief that all cops were decent and intelligent.

I was posted to the Northern Division of Glasgow, based in Maitland Street. It had numerous tough areas and I was involved in many a fracas, as were all working cops in a busy division. My tutors and colleagues were men who had served in the Second World War and, having come through that experience, were entirely unfazed by what the Glasgow neds could throw at them. I learned from them very quickly and found I could be as tough as the people I faced. In those days, it was only men who were on the beat. Although there were a small number of policewomen in the Glasgow City Police, they were office-based unless they were called upon to deal with domestic incidents, sexual assaults or crimes against children.

During my stint in uniform, I received my first commendation from the Chief Constable, Sir James Robertson, for apprehending a violent housebreaker on one of the first nights of my night-shift stint, which then lasted for six weeks. I was patrolling in the St George's Road area with an older colleague, Harry Lappin, when we heard the sound of glass breaking coming from New City Road, where there were a number of large shops. Both of us immediately started to run in the direction of the sound. Being younger and fitter, I left Harry trailing and as I got there I saw two young hooligans running away from a broken plate-glass window at the Co-operative department store. Both were carrying large objects that later turned out to be reel-to-reel tape recorders, which in the early 1960s were the ultimate in recording technology. Each was the size of a small suitcase. I chased the youths and one of them dropped what he was carrying before taking off. The other one was reluctant to relinquish his grip on his booty, so I managed to get closer to him and eventually cornered him in a common close. I got him by the scruff of the neck and dragged him back to the shop, where we awaited the arrival of my colleagues.

What I didn't know was that he stayed directly above the shop with his family. He started to shout and fight, punching and kicking like mad while I tried to keep a hold of him. As this was going on, his sister came down from their house and started laying into the back of my head with a stiletto shoe. I can assure you this was quite sore. Luckily, the divisional patrol car appeared in the street and assisted me in arresting both the housebreaker and his sister. He subsequently received three months for the housebreaking. Within six months of being released, this ned turned his attention to robbing a bookmaker's shop in the Shettleston area of Glasgow. He armed himself with a large butcher's knife and used this on the proprietor, cutting off three of his fingers.

I disliked uniform duties – I found them mundane and not as I had imagined. I was attracted to plain-clothes duty, which I was drafted into after my probationary period of two years was complete, and I became a fully fledged 'plainer' (plain-clothes man) after three years' service.

I did not understand that at this time some older cops did not want plain-clothes duty simply because betting shops had been legalised. Prior to this, bookies had apparently been a source of revenue for unscrupulous 'plainers', who had the duty of identifying and dealing with these illegal premises and could make money from tipping off the bookies when a raid was about to take place. I personally did not know anyone involved in these activities, although I was aware that it had taken place. In plain clothes I saw the prospect of hard work, which suited me fine, because if you had a good colleague – or 'neighbour' – and bosses who backed you up, you were able to work proactively in a manner where you could be effective against the criminals.

The plain-clothes era of my career was great fun and it really opened my young eyes. My steady neighbour was initially Davy Frew, a few years older than me and at this time much wiser, which was just as well. Our remit was to concentrate on catching car thieves, housebreakers and a variety of other street criminals but also, through our various contacts, we had to attempt to identify the locations of brothels and shebeens (unlicensed drinking dens). These last activities were particularly encouraged by our shift inspector, because if you managed to mount a successful operation on that type of premises then the inspector would have to submit a report to the Chief Constable. His report would highlight his own name, perhaps useful for further promotion. There are always wheels within wheels in police work.

One day, a shopkeeper from Balornock housing scheme had requested an interview with our inspector, Albert Provan. He recounted that he had just found religion and as a consequence wished to use Albert as his father confessor regarding his continual use of a particular brothel within our area.

The inspector called us in and told us to begin observations on a two-storey flat in St Peter's Street, off New City Road, which he alleged was being used by a number of women during the afternoon to ply their trade. These were not street girls. They stayed in the house waiting for clients to book their various services by phone. Because the trade took place during daylight hours, Davy and I realised it was going to be a wee bit difficult to keep the place under observation without ourselves being observed. In those days, plainers did not have unlimited access to vehicles and if we just hung about in the street we would have stood out like sore thumbs. Davy came up with the idea of approaching some of the local house factors to find out if there were any vacant premises that we could use for a few days. We were extremely lucky and found a flat almost directly opposite the target that could be used as our observation post, or OP. Even better, it was fully furnished so we were able to draw a couple of large easy chairs over to the windows, a touch of pure luxury compared to most stakeouts. From our vantage point, we could clock everything that was taking place in the relatively short street.

We were very surprised by the amount of traffic going in and out of the flat. Many of the clients obligingly arrived in their private cars, which they parked in the street. Their number plates were duly noted so their owners could be contacted later and get a wee surprise! Another definite giveaway was the fact that the knocking shop had two windows to the front – both of which had their curtains drawn. Usually, when their customers were leaving the close, the ladies would appear at the windows, wave them farewell and blow them a goodbye kiss. I don't know if that cost extra.

On the first day, we saw a beautiful two-tone Jaguar drawing up and a rotund, bald-headed, elderly man limp into the close. He reappeared about 45 minutes later and received his goodbye wave from the window but did not climb back into his car. Instead, he made his way on foot towards New City Road. We decided I would leave the OP and follow, to see where he was heading. He went straight to the nearest pub, where he downed an extremely large brandy.

Three days of observations were necessary for this type of case in order that a pattern of behaviour could be established, before we could apply to a sheriff for a warrant for the house in question. For us, it was simply a matter of noting the comings and goings (so to speak) and the registration numbers of cars. Business was brisk and the man in the lovely Jag showed up every day and afterwards headed for the same New City Road pub.

Our inspector now set about obtaining a warrant. Davy and I appeared before a sheriff in private chambers, where we swore under oath to the veracity of our observations. Once armed with official sanction, we planned to hit the place that afternoon. The general yardstick was to ensure that there were at least two punters and two hookers in any brothel before a raid. As there always seemed to be at least four women 'on duty' in the house, we hoped that the wee punter in the Jaguar would appear again, then all we would need was one more client to arrive. Uniformed officers with the inspector and sergeant were around the corner in an unmarked van waiting for the word from us to go.

Davy and I knew that our observations were crucial, so we decided to take turns going into the close opposite to ensure that 'customers' were in fact entering the target house. We tossed a coin to see which of us would be very close to the action and be in the building when hopefully the next punter appeared. I won the toss and got the job, a big deal for a relatively young and inexperienced officer. That day, I had turned up to appear before the sheriff for the craving of the warrant in my collar, tie and smart suit but at lunchtime I changed into denims, a combat jacket and casual shirt for my undercover role, quite unusual at this time, because as a plain-clothes man you were expected to turn out for work like a tailor's dummy!

The wait was on for the punters to appear before we swung into action. Like clockwork, the two-tone Jaguar drove into the street and our friend entered the close. I heard him go up to the door and be allowed in. We were now waiting for a second customer to appear. We did not have long to wait. Another car drove into the street and its occupant went into the close. I crossed the street and climbed the stairs to the first landing, hoping to get a glimpse of the man going into our target house. I was too eager and bumped into him on the stairs – he was still at the door of the whorehouse – so I just continued past him up to the next landing and banged on a door, praying that no one would answer it. I was in luck. No one did, and the punter went into the house. I then ran to the close entrance to signal my colleagues. We had no personal radios in those days so the signal was the waving of a dirty white handkerchief. The troops came running down the street to join me and we hurried upstairs. We had already obtained a plan of the house from the city council offices and had made sure we knew where we were heading once we gained entry. This was achieved by applying a policeman's size nine to the door. I took the first door to the right; and there in this bedroom was the man I had bumped into on the stairs. He was already in a state of undress on a bed and being entertained to a striptease performance by a young lady while he was trying to put on a condom but not having lots of luck because of his shaking hands.

The real action was taking place in the main front room, where we found our Jaguar friend with a woman. He was standing naked from the waist down with his little shirt tail tucked up, his ankles bound together and his hands tied in front of him. The lady, clad in her underwear, was also wearing a large wooden voodoo mask and wielding a cat-of-nine-tails, which she was in the process of applying to his podgy buttocks. Each to his own! Later, while giving his statement, he revealed that he was only 42 years old. We had pegged him at much older. It turned out his limp was due to the regular administration of the lash. So much for sex being good for your health. No wonder he needed a very large brandy after each session.

There were five women in the house at this time, none known prostitutes. They were all married women earning pin money while their husbands were presumably out earning an honest crust. While we were still in the house, another two punters turned up and were welcomed with open arms – but by the police, not the hookers. The house was littered with a variety of masks and whips, ranging from soft leather belts to more lethal-looking flagellation instruments such as solid wooden batons, riding crops and the cat-of-nine-tails that we had seen earlier.

The John Profumo scandal was raging at this time. Profumo was a Tory government cabinet minister who became involved with call girls and attended wild parties, where, it was reported, flagellation cost around £1 per stroke, bringing the average price for a session to £50. In the St Peter's Street whorehouse, you could get a real doing for a fiver!

The hookers and their equipment were escorted to Maitland Street, where statements were obtained. The householder was charged with running a brothel. While taking a statement from one of the women, I naively asked if she enjoyed her work, to which she replied, 'It's so much fun, son, if I had another pair of legs I'd open in Edinburgh!'

The equipment taken from that house of ill repute spent many years in the Glasgow Police Museum.

ASSAULT WITH A WOODEN LEG

During my two-year spell in plain clothes, I received a further five commendations for arresting neds in connection with a variety of crimes. Without radios, you were more or less on your own apart from having a good neighbour, a baton, handcuffs and a whistle. In a radio interview a few years ago, I said you did not use your baton unless your life was threatened and it was pointless trying to blow your whistle when your teeth were being kicked out. This sounded quite funny but it was true.

Another vital weapon in the police armoury in those days was the police box. Now best known through *Doctor Who*, the police box fulfilled a number of functions. Inside was a phone that could be used by stations to contact the officer on the beat. The light above flashed when there was a call that needed attention. The beat men also used the phone to report in or call for assistance. The box itself was a handy place to shelter from inclement weather, to store snacks or even something strong to keep out the chill of a night shift on the streets. It was while trying to use the facilities of a city-centre box that I managed to get my nose broken. And by an artificial leg, no less.

One day, I was in plain clothes working the back shift, from 2 p.m. to 11 p.m. along with my colleague Stuart Burnett. We were operating in the area around Renfrew Street, in the city centre, when we were approached by a woman who worked in a nearby café frequented by unsavoury characters, prostitutes and pimps. Knowing that we were police officers, she sidled up to us and started speaking in a low tone from the side of her mouth.

'There's a bloke inside that you might want to take a look at,' she said.

I asked, 'What's wrong, hen?'

'He's a right bad bastard – and he's got a dirty great big butcher's knife stuck in his trousers.'

'Do you know who he is?'

'Aye – it's "Sticky" Carr.'

Stuart and I looked at each other. We both knew we were in for a tough time. 'Sticky' was a pimp who was well known to the local police. He was called 'Sticky' because he had a wooden leg and used a walking stick. He was a violent man with a wicked temper and he hated the police. Coming along quietly was not a phrase in his vocabulary. Luckily, we were spotted as we entered the café by two beat cops who realised that help might be required and so positioned themselves in the doorway. Not standing on ceremony, Stuart and I grabbed hold of Carr and took the knife from him before he had any chance of pulling it. The woman who had approached us had been mistaken, it was not a dirty, great, big knife – it was a dirty, great, big, *enormous* knife.

The next problem was to get Carr from the café to the nearby police box in Hope Street, where we could hold him until transportation arrived. We knew that whenever he was about to be arrested, Carr, who was a big man, would fall to the ground and be as awkward as possible. This is where our two uniformed colleagues came in handy and together we carried him bodily round to the police box. However, we could not get him inside, so the struggle continued on the pavement. Matters were further complicated by the fact that it was now 10 p.m. and the local pubs were emptying. Although Stuart had managed to phone from the box for the van to attend, our efforts to contain the still struggling 'Sticky' were now being observed by a large and hostile crowd.

The four of us were each trying to control a limb. I had an arm, as had Stuart, while the two uniform cops held a leg each. The younger of these two cops had recently joined us from the army but despite that he did not appreciate the rough and tumble of police work. (He had attained the nickname of 'the galloping major'.) He was attempting to hold Carr's artificial leg, which had strong springs at the knee and ankle joints. I turned towards 'the major' to encourage him to hold on tightly, just as he let go. The leg was thrashing about wildly as if it had a life of its own and suddenly sprang towards me, kicking me solidly on the face. My nose burst wide open and spilled blood all over the place. The crowd then fled, not because they couldn't stand the sight of blood but because they had spotted a police van arriving. My nose was broken in two places and my suit was ruined. In those days, you wouldn't have dared to ask the force to pay the cleaning costs.

Carr was duly locked up and charged with a breach of the peace, police assault and being in possession of two offensive weapons, one being the knife, the other being a really horrible and dangerous leg!

GEORGE HARRISON'S JAGUAR

One dark evening, on my way home after a thirty-mile run on my bicycle, I was passing a car saleroom close to my house, when I noticed that one of the large plate-glass windows on the forecourt had been smashed. Sitting just inside the showroom close to the broken window was a white E-Type Jaguar which was quite a point of interest in Glasgow, as it had apparently been owned by the Beatle George Harrison. It was a lucrative sideline for the entrepreneurial garage owner, who was charging five pounds for a short ride in it.

I cycled into the forecourt and spotted a man sitting in the driver's seat of the Jaguar. I dropped my bike, climbed through the broken garage window and approached the ned in the car. In true Glasgow parlance, I said to him, 'I'm a cop and you're getting the jail.' He was somewhat taken aback but slid out from behind the wheel quietly. We both climbed back out through the broken window and I marched him along to Springburn Police Station in Hawthorn Street. As we walked along, I asked him, 'What the hell were you planning to do with the car?'

He said, 'If I'd managed to get it started, I was gonnae take it for a wee hurl.'

'How were you going to get it out of the showroom?'

He looked at me as if I was daft and said, as if it was the most obvious thing in the world, 'I was gonnae drive it through the windae!'

Given the local fame of the vehicle, this plan to take it 'for a wee hurl' and save himself a fiver sounded fair enough. The problem was, I'd also noticed that he had loaded the car with other goodies from the garage.

My companion received the customary warm welcome from the duty sergeant at Springburn and was given a room without a view for the night. Accompanied by other cops, I returned to the garage and was pleased to see that my bike was still there. Unfortunately, I had sustained a front-wheel puncture from the broken glass. I left the officers standing by the garage while I walked back to Springburn Police Station, carrying my bike. The duty sergeant told me that I would have to go to the divisional headquarters at Maitland Street to give a statement to the CID. I was fortunate enough to get a lift there in the back of the divisional Land Rover. I was still dressed in my wet, sweaty cycling gear, so I was not a pretty sight nor particularly fragrant.

On arriving at Maitland Street, I went into the detective sergeant's room to complete my statement. During this process, the room suddenly filled with a number of detectives I had never set eyes on before. Apparently, a fight had started in a local house and when I heard the name of the occupants it immediately caught my attention. As previously explained, part of my duties as a plain-clothes officer entailed looking for and identifying shebeens and brothels, both of which were considered as houses of ill repute. This house and its occupants were on my list and I had taken observations on the comings and goings there only the day before. Subsequent to this, three unwelcome guests had entered the house. They had been confronted by a young member of the family and told to leave; as a result, they had dragged this 16-year-old boy onto the landing outside the house, closed the door and stabbed him to death. As I listened to this story, I heard the name Boyle being mentioned as one of the suspects. I was aware that there was a Jimmy Boyle who was known to have close associations with the prostitutes who frequented that area.

I turned to the detectives, who were from the Flying Squad, and told them that I knew of Boyle and his associates, specifically three girls, and named them, but they started to pooh-pooh this information and were very dismissive, which annoyed me. I told them they could do what they liked but my information was correct. While this conversation was going on, an older man walked into the room and stood at the door. This turned out to be the legendary Tom Goodall, head of Glasgow CID, who was to become something of a nemesis to Jimmy Boyle. He said very quietly but forcefully to the members of the Flying Squad team, 'Listen to what this laddie has to say, because it's more than any of you lot are offering.' I wrote down my information and left it with them. I later put one of the local detectives in touch with a prostitute who eventually came up with the information that Boyle was holed up in Maryhill and he was arrested there. He and others stood trial for this murder but Boyle was cleared.

Tom Goodall was an amazing officer and was in charge of some of the best detectives in Scotland, but he could never remember many of the younger officers' names, therefore, he referred to them all as 'Laddie'. This was the first time I met up with him. It would not be the last.

CID BECKONS

I was identified as CID material because I had earned a reputation as a good thief catcher and someone to be relied upon, as opposed to the sort of police officer who simply talked a good game and had neither the ability nor the inclination to back up his boasts with appropriate actions. Although I thoroughly enjoyed plain clothes, my aim was to become a detective. I thought that all detective officers were superhuman but I was soon to learn that a lot of them had achieved their ranks with the use of funny handshakes rather than handcuffs. Be that as it may, I got the opportunity to work with some truly great detectives and was involved in many fascinating cases, some high profile.

On joining the CID, I had an interview with Tom Goodall, who personally vetted every officer that applied, and also one with my chief superintendent, Mr Curdy, a real tough old cop who told me he did not want me sitting at a desk all day – I should be out locking up criminals. Exactly what I wanted to hear. Mr Goodall laid down strict rules. He said he did not want to hear of any 'graft'. This took me by surprise – for a moment I thought he meant hard work. Of course, he was talking about backhanders. To become part of this elite group, I had to go and buy myself a soft hat. There was no uniform for CID officers but they had to have a hat. Tom Goodall, who was well known to the public, was never seen without his hat and his pipe. This hat malarkey always seemed a bit silly to me, as it immediately identified people as CID officers. It was really a status symbol. However, the only choice left to me was whether it would be a fedora, trilby or soft bowler. I plumped for a corduroy number but I rarely wore it and it occupied a more or less permanent position on a peg in the CID office.

I had been selected for the CID partly because of the quality of my informants, or touts, one of whom steered me information that helped me clear up a lot of crimes all over the city after I became a detective. One case involved the recovery of a full container-load of cigarettes that had been heisted from the Lothian area. The Edinburgh force tended to work with insurance companies, whereas Glasgow did not, but on this occasion a reward of £500 was forwarded for my tout – a lot of money in the 1960s. Mr Goodall told me to bring my man in to receive it. I was taken aback at this, because on a CID training course I had been lectured on the perils of revealing your touts' identities. The man delivering the lecture had been DCS Tom Goodall. However, an order was an order. I brought the man in. We found the corridor lined with Flying Squad officers, all desperate for a look at him. Mr Goodall sent me away to type out a receipt for the money. When I returned, the reward had been handed over and I took my man away again. On the way out, he told me that Mr Goodall had tried to 'sign him on' – in other words, poach him for himself. It was clear that even bosses – however legendary – were not above trying to pull strokes for their own personal advantage.

It was a tout, although not one of mine, who told us that there was going to be a hold-up at a bank near the high flats in Royston Road. According to the information, neds were going to rob a blacksmith's in Dobbies Loan. The owner, James Allan, accompanied by one of his staff as bodyguard, collected his workers' wages every Friday morning from the bank. When we got wind of the hold-up, my bosses thought up a cunning plan in which a detective officer disguised in dirty overalls and a flat cap would accompany Mr Allan instead. Other officers were to be positioned around the flats, while two enterprising policewomen donned curlers, headscarves and overalls and stayed close by, with their batons inside their message bags.

Either because I was the newest recruit, or because my experience as a plasterer meant I was suited to the costume, it was me the bosses decided to kit out in overalls and with a suitably dirty face. We employed very sophisticated protective gear in those days: aware that the gang would be armed with baseball bats, one of my bosses kindly lent me his copy of the *Daily Worker* to put inside my cap in case I was walloped during the raid. Perhaps he thought its heavy communist leanings would make it more resilient than, say, the *Daily Record*. Fortunately, the theory was never put to the test. I returned with Mr Allan to his business premises after our run to the bank, by which time it was obvious no raid was going to take place, quickly cleaned myself up and returned with him to collect the wages.

Although we did not make any arrests on this occasion, we probably did foil the raid by causing the villains to change their plans when they realised that the bodyguard was someone new. Mr Allan was effusive in his praise for the police and as a token of his gratitude tried to present me with three pencils with the name of his company emblazoned upon them. I refused this kind offer, as it was not something that could be drunk by the rest of the troops!

BOBO AND MAU-MAU

Blackhill was a rough area and violence was common on its streets. A report came in that a middle-aged man had been mugged, stabbed through the heart and left for dead in a common close in Acrehill Street. We learned from local residents that Robert 'Bobo' Murney and

William 'Mau-Mau' Morrison, a pair of dangerous teenage thugs, were responsible. According to information received, Murney sometimes carried a gun. Six of us headed for Castlemilk and threw a cordon around his ground-floor flat. I was given the job of kicking in the door, the warrant being contained in the sole of my left boot. (In other words, we didn't have one!) Inside we found a young woman breastfeeding her baby, but no sign of Bobo. We settled down to wait for him and, lo and behold, the bold boy came merrily home from his work with the Cleansing Department. All he was carrying was his piece-box.

On being locked up, Bobo obligingly warned us to be careful with Mau-Mau, who, he said, was always armed, at the very least with a knife. DI Harry Watts, DS Gordon Cameron, DC 'Big' John MacDonald and I went to the top-floor flat in Blackhill where the Morrison boy lived with his parents. Again, the suspect was not at home – like his pal Bobo, he was out at work. (This was the first and last time that I came upon two genuinely working neds.) The bosses stayed in the house with Morrison's parents while Big John and I waited outside, I on the first-floor landing, John across the street. We planned to trap Mau-Mau in the close. It was not advisable to run through back courts in Blackhill, where they were known to dig elephant traps for unsuspecting police officers. In fact, it was never a good idea to go careering around in the dark, as all sorts of hazards lay in wait for pursuing cops – my brother John was once nearly decapitated by a clothes wire. Your quarry knew where the traps were and avoided them.

Darkness fell. At about 6 p.m. I heard footsteps. A figure started to come up the stairs. When he came into view, I saw he fitted our man's description. I also saw that he had a weapon in his hand, a vicious-looking blade with a serrated edge. He had obviously been expecting trouble and was more prepared than I was. Before I could say anything, he came straight at me, swinging the blade. His first blow sliced my coat at my chest. He turned to run but I was after him and had pulled out my baton. He was slightly below me on the stairs and I aimed it at his napper, skelping him twice on the top of his head, causing his green Celtic cap to turn the colour of a Hearts jersey. He dropped to his knees with the force of the blows.

When John had seen Mau-Mau with the blade, he threw up his hands in a defensive gesture. Mau-Mau started to get up and turned back towards me, and I launched myself at him. John and I both piled in and finally managed to wrest the blade from his hands. We then took him up to his house, where his wounds were treated by DS Cameron, who, as an emergency first-aid measure, retrieved a grey dishcloth from under the sink and applied it to Mau-Mau's skull. John and I then took him to the Royal Infirmary, where a doctor sewed 18 sutures into his head, making a lovely centre parting.

While we waited at the Royal, I asked Mau-Mau why he had turned to face me again, between blows so to speak. 'Why didn't you keep going at my neighbour, since he'd not managed to draw his baton?'

Mau-Mau replied, 'I'm not stupid – I know karate when I see it.'

He thought John's hands going up had meant he was taking a martial arts stance, when, in fact, he was just about to shit himself – as was I when we saw the weapon in Mau-Mau's hands, which was a blade from a mechanical saw, one side serrated, the other finely honed. The grip had been fashioned from black electrical tape. A fearsome weapon indeed.

This case finished up at the High Court. Mau-Mau was represented by a frequent adversary of mine in this particular arena, Nicholas Fairbairn QC. After I had given my Evidence-in-Chief under questioning by the Advocate Depute acting for the Crown, it was Fairbairn's chance to have a go at me. The questioning went something like this:

'What height are you, Detective Constable?'

'I'm just about five foot ten,' I replied, wondering where this was leading.

'And what is the length of your baton?'

I took it that he was referring to my police baton.

'Approximately ten inches long,' I said, still unable to work out where he was going with these questions.

'And can you tell me the height of my client, Mr Morrison?'

'About five foot eight.'

'And are you aware of the length of the weapon allegedly wielded by my client?'

'The blade would be about seven inches.'

'So it was not a very fair fight that evening, was it? You are a taller man and were in possession of a much larger weapon . . .'

I couldn't believe what I was hearing. Fairbairn then went on to quote the Glasgow Police Instruction Manual regarding the use of the police baton. It told us that an officer should strike his attacker on the shoulders or legs but never on the head.

'That's true,' I agreed, 'that's what the manual says. But I wasn't in possession of the manual on that night in Blackhill. My aim for the head was done in order to disarm and arrest a violent young criminal.'

I honestly could not understand Fairbairn's line of questioning on this occasion; nor did he impress the judge or jury. He was just digging a deeper hole for his client. Both the accused got five years for the stabbing. (The unfortunate victim died some six months later.) Mau-Mau got a sore head and a further three years for having a go at me with the saw blade.

FUN WITH DOG TURDS

One of my earliest CID neighbours was a chap called John McVicar. John was an excellent cop, one of the best, and full of practical jokes. At lunchtime, he liked nothing better than nipping down to Tam Shepherd's Joke Shop in Queen Street to see if there were any new tricks he could buy.

When he was in Central Division, he was the van driver for a short period. This duty, as well as collecting prisoners, also entailed looking after the stray animals that were handed in from time to time and placed in the kennels at the office. John, being John, found this a very dull tour of duty and decided to spice it up. He placed a dummy dog turd near the duty inspector's desk, making it all the more realistic by covering it with steaming hot tea. He said that a dog that he'd had to bring through the bar area had left it there. The inspector went off the deep end when he saw it and gave John a bollocking, telling him to get rid of the stinking mess. John surprised him by apparently picking up the offending poo with his bare hands. Then the inspector realised he had been conned and they all had a good chuckle.

The inspector decided to play the same joke on the divisional commander, who was due to come into the office, so he asked John to set it up again. However, John, again being John, slightly changed the joke by going to the kennels and retrieving a real dog crap, which he placed on the floor. The divisional commander came in shortly afterwards and on seeing the mess told the inspector in no uncertain terms to get it cleaned. The inspector, copying John's earlier actions, calmly bent down and stuck his hand deep into a pile of steaming shit. The divisional commander was not amused. The inspector was none too pleased either.

Needless to say, John never worked as van driver on that particular inspector's shift again and spent the rest of that day driving in circles around the division rather than going back to face the wrath of the inspector.

BACK TO BLACKHILL

Around 1967, due to the amount of information I was receiving and crimes I was solving as a detective at Maitland Street, I was transferred to the Glasgow Flying Squad – supposedly the crème de la crème. I thought it would be wonderful. It was, in fact, one of the worst periods in my service. The Flying Squad was based on the London model – a team of detectives who could tackle serious crime across the force area without a care for divisional boundaries. At this time, there were eight divisions in Glasgow and Flying Squad officers were drawn from each one. There were three individual squads, each made up of an inspector, two sergeants and a constable – or rather, the tea boy. I didn't take too well to the role. I made rotten tea.

Many's the time on night shift I would be driving with one particular sergeant sleeping on the back seat after having consumed two fish suppers and a bottle of Irn-Bru. The gastric effects of this combination were pretty toxic. There were, however, some good detectives in the squad, as some divisions thought highly of it and sent their best officers on secondment. Others offloaded their worst men to it. As a result, there was a frustrating lack of consistency in the quality of its work and the freeloaders were always trying to avoid the tasks they were allocated.

I never really settled into the Flying Squad and in late 1967 was relieved to return to the Northern Division, where my one-time neighbour, John 'the Joker' McVicar, had risen to the rank of detective chief inspector and was in charge of the CID. The North was still the North, with lots of serious crime taking place, and John, due to his leadership qualities and the calibre of his staff, continued to enjoy the highest clear-up rate in the city.

One Saturday night, I was off duty, supposedly for the weekend, when I received a call instructing me to attend at the office first thing on Sunday morning. There had been a murder in Provanmill Road just outside the Provanmill Inn, a real rapscallion's pub frequented by Blackhill and Provanmill ne'er do wells and villains. More chibs were carried in this pub than halves of whisky drunk.

The murder, which had been committed at about 9.30 p.m., was the latest episode in a longstanding feud between two Blackhill families, the 'Smiths' and the 'Joneses'. The background was that about four months earlier, there had been a knife fight in the Provanmill Inn, in which the young Smith had been stabbed. After he was discharged from hospital, he went to stay with his wife's family in Possilpark, where he licked his wounds and contemplated revenge. His assailant remained in Blackhill but had stayed clear of the local hostelries, lying low until he felt that everything had cooled down.

The young Smith stayed well clear and so everything seemed hunky-dory, but that is not the way it works in Blackhill. He had his spies out in the pubs, waiting for Jones to re-appear. Sure enough, Jones emerged from his lair. Saturday night in Blackhill – it's either the loneliest night of the week or it's all right for fighting, depending on your age and taste in songs. For Jones, it was to be the last Saturday night he would ever see.

Smith got the phone call he'd been waiting for, telling him that his opponent had just arrived at the Provanmill Inn and was ordering his first pint. Smith set off for the pub but did not enter. One of his spies had told him that Jones was by then on his third pint and was also downing whisky chasers. Clearly his long period of abstinence was over. Smith decided to bide his time.

Jones finally left the Inn well puggled. As he staggered along Provanmill Road, he stopped to relieve himself – and that was when Smith made his move. He plunged a large knife twice into Jones's chest and, as he was right-handed, both blows struck the drunk man on the left side of his body. A pathologist later explained to me that this form of attack – a right-handed strike face-on to a victim – accounts for many fatal stab wounds to the heart. Jones staggered a few steps, then collapsed. The blows had been savage and fatal.

People from Blackhill would certainly report murders – after all, it was easy in those days to make an anonymous call from a public phone box – but when it came to giving any relevant information, it was a different story. That could lead to them appearing in court and being called upon to speak up against their neighbours, and that was just not on. That could lead to a fate worse than death. The Sicilians call it *omerta* but in Glasgow it's called *keepin' your fuckin' mouth shut*. This is the problem DCI McVicar was faced with.

John swiftly appraised himself of the sequence leading to the murder but he was having serious difficulty finding witnesses to the killing. However, as the one-time head of Glasgow CID, Elphinstone Maitland Dalgleish, used to preach to new CID recruits, 'Get the body [accused] and we'll get the evidence.' It may be a harsh philosophy but nine times out of ten it works. Once you had the body in custody, people were more likely to speak to the police, as they did not feel as if they were firing anyone in if they were already locked up. In this case, everyone knew Smith had plunged his rival and he was duly hoovered up.

We still required a lot more evidence. It needed a lot of fast work to ensure that as much relevant evidence as possible was gathered before presentation of the case to the Procurator Fiscal. Before John McVicar went for a few hours of much-needed rest, he left instructions for door-to-door inquiries to be undertaken in the area surrounding the killing and in the neighbourhood of the victim's home.

I was one of the detectives pounding the streets and banging the doors. Like my colleagues, I was getting nowhere – until I spoke to a neighbour of the Jones family who told me that a teenage girl and her younger sister had witnessed the killing. The neighbour said that the girls knew both the murdered man and his assailant. Hoping that this tip wasn't a load of bollocks, I spoke to the girls. Much to my delight and surprise, these two were the kinds of witnesses a cop dreams of. The older girl was so aware of the animosity between the feuding families that when she saw the two men coming together her first thought was, 'That's Smith making his big move now.' The events of that Saturday night were totally expected in Blackhill – and were, to an extent, regarded as acceptable.

From the girls' statements, we were able to trace other eyewitnesses and tie up the inquiry so that when DCI McVicar came back on duty the following afternoon he had everything presented to him in a neat and tidy bundle. John was more than pleased and I thought we would be able to relax and bask in the reflected glory of our effort. Not a bit of it. He decided to put me off my dinner by sending me to represent him at the post-mortem examination at the Glasgow mortuary. But rather than putting me off my dinner, I found the whole process quite enlightening. The pathologist, seeing that I was comparatively new to this particular facet of police work, went to great lengths to show me the route the knife had taken into the heart of the victim and how measurement of the wound could reveal the length of the weapon used.

Sometimes I did find it a gruesome experience attending post-mortem examinations. It all depended on the attitude of the pathologists. I remember a very pretty blonde pathologist telling me, while pulling at the intestines of a cadaver, that she was looking forward to having spaghetti bolognese for lunch. Thankfully, she did not mention having a 'nice bottle of Chianti' as she sucked at her bottom lip.

I was present at one post-mortem where, as happened in those days, the mortuary attendant was given the task of removing the top of the skull. He peeled back the scalp, sliced open the skull with a circular saw and lifted out the brain, which was examined by the surgeon and then placed in an ordinary plastic basin ready for dissection. Other organs were also removed, including the heart, liver and lungs, to be dissected by the pathologists in order to be completely satisfied as to the cause of death. It was then down to the mortuary attendant to clean up and make the body as presentable as possible. The chap, who was new to the job, was having quite a bit of trouble marrying up the newly removed top of the skull with the lower half. The two pieces refused to stay in place, because the brain cavity was now empty. The pathologist solved the problem by crumpling up two or three sheets of newspaper and jamming them into the hole. He commented that the dead man on the slab now had more intelligence in his head than he ever had when he was living. The organs, including the brain, were then all placed together into a large black bin bag, which was deposited into the stomach cavity of the corpse before being crudely stitched up by the mortuary attendant.

More than a few hardbitten detectives have left the Glasgow mortuary feeling queasy and swearing to lead a better life in order to die quietly, hopefully in their own beds, so that there would be no need for any type of post-mortem!

MORE FAMILY MATTERS

The reason I was sent back to Northern Division was that during my stint in the Flying Squad I separated from my first wife – divorce was frowned upon within the police force and could even be a barrier to advancement. I was 20 and Rena 19 years of age when we married. We were far too young to have any real sense of what it was about. During our eight years together, we had two girls, Laura and Kirsty.

I left the family home soon after Kirsty was born. She was too young to realise what was happening but Laura, who was five, took the split very hard. Due to varying shift patterns, I could not see the girls every weekend as I would have liked and after a while Rena suggested that seeing them irregularly like this was causing Laura too much heartache and she wasn't settling after her visits with me, so it might be better if I did not see them again. I reluctantly agreed. Rena later remarried a chap named John Young and my daughters changed their second name. Both have gone on to have highly successful careers, Kirsty as a TV broadcaster and presenter. I have followed her progress with great interest.

However, Laura was little more than a baby when I had my first brush with the man the media later called the Godfather of Glasgow.

The Arthur Thompson Saga

The police always knew Arthur Thompson as a right handful. Like me, he hailed from the East End of the city but, unlike me, he was classed as a very violent and ruthless criminal. Add to this the fact that he was intelligent and you had a very dangerous mix. His first conviction was in 1949, when, aged 18, he was fined for assault. Over the following years, he built his record and his reputation with robbery, extortion and reset (what Scots law calls receiving stolen property). He was buddies with legendary, or notorious, safecrackers 'Gentle Johnny' Ramensky and Paddy Meehan. It was with Meehan that he blew a hole in a Beauly bank safe, a caper for which he did two years. Thompson's name was enough to strike fear into anyone who crossed him.

As Britain moved into the swinging '60s, he took a step back from pulling jobs himself and became a criminal executive, if you will. He added to his income by money-lending and operating illegal casinos. (As a plain-clothes officer, I was involved in a raid on one of his gambling dens, The Raven, situated in a lane in Glasgow's city centre. As well as arresting everyone involved, we stripped the premises of anything related to illegal gaming, including roulette wheels, gambling tables and even wall drapes.) Thompson was deeply involved in protection rackets, which included putting the squeeze on breweries that had pubs in his area. He even managed to have his wife down on the books of one of these pubs as a 'singer', with a fee of £200 for each performance, probably more than Cilla Black was getting at the time. In fact, as far as I know, Rita Thompson never sang a note in public – the fee was merely camouflage in the books for the protection they paid to Thompson.

In addition to all his nefarious activities, Thompson was involved in a number of legitimate business concerns, including scrap-metal dealerships, car salerooms, a timber outlet and a joinery firm, the latter of which was for many years his only recorded source of income.

Thompson had heavy connections in London, most notably the infamous Kray twins, Ronnie and Reggie. It was well known that Arthur regularly took the first early-morning flight down to London in order to do jobs for the Krays, coming back up on a later flight when the job was completed. What a great cover for a hit man. If the twins were looking for someone with plenty of bottle and no scruples to back them up, they certainly had their man in Arthur Thompson. It is rumoured he was present when Ronnie Kray shot George Cornell of the rival Richardson gang in the Blind Beggar pub in Whitechapel in March 1966.

Little did I realise that my first confrontation with him would almost end the careers of both my brother John and myself before they had properly begun and put us on the front page of every daily newspaper in Scotland.

John was working in uniform in the East End of Glasgow and, whenever possible, we would get together to socialise and talk shop. When he tore ligaments in his leg after chasing some criminals on a railway line, this coincided with my having the unusual luxury of a

Saturday night off and we decided to go for a beer in a hotel in the village of Stepps on the northern outskirts of Glasgow – neither of us would ever drink in a pub in the city, a practice that was common amongst police officers due to the risk of a confrontation with some aggrieved villain.

That evening in May 1966, as we were heading out of the city we spotted a Mark 10 Jaguar having a tussle with a small white Morris van. As John and I sat at the junction of Red Road and Royston Road, we watched the vehicles speed past. About 100 yards further on, the van careered into the stone parapet of a railway bridge, bounced off and wrapped itself around a concrete light standard. The Jaguar screeched away and turned off into a petrol station further down the road.

I already knew who the driver was. As the Jaguar had come towards the junction, I had got a clear view of Arthur Thompson behind the wheel.

I leapt out of our car and rushed over to the wrecked vehicle. John, partly crippled by his leg injury, limped along behind me. We did not need a doctor to tell us that the two guys inside were dead. There was debris and petrol all over the tarmac, leaving the surface in a very dangerous condition and quite a few people were milling about trying to assist. A bus travelling citywards stopped and the driver told me he had witnessed the two vehicles having a go at each other. John stayed with the van, while I ran towards the petrol station I'd seen Thompson's car drawing into.

When I reached the garage, Thompson was standing by himself on the forecourt. I ran up to him and said, 'Arthur, you stay here, I want a word with you.' I'd never had direct dealings with him before but there was not a cop in the city who did not know him and I am sure he knew I was a police officer. I then went into the kiosk to phone police control for much-needed backup as well as the fire brigade and ambulance. While I was phoning, Thompson drove off. This did not worry me unduly, as I knew he lived nearby. Later, I was told that he had been in possession of a gun when I confronted him. Knowing his reputation, I was probably lucky he did decide to bugger off. I went back to the wrecked van and waited. Tommy Munn, the detective sergeant on duty that night, arrived at the scene and took control.

After John and I had told him what had happened and what we had seen and done, he ordered us to go to nearby Maitland Street and we spent the rest of that night completing statements and other paperwork at the Northern Police Office. So much for the chance of a quiet beer together.

The driver of the Morris van was James Goldie, his passenger a local hard man, Patrick Welsh – both bitter rivals of Thompson. Earlier in the evening, they had been drinking in the Forge Bar in Forge Street, not far from the scene of the 'accident'. Goldie had placed a bet earlier in the day at the local bookies, the owner of which paid Thompson for protection. Goldie left the pub to collect his winnings and there was a slight altercation between him and the bookie over the exact amount he should have received. Goldie returned to the pub and asked Welsh to accompany him back to press his case in a more forceful manner.

The row escalated somewhat. The two men eventually received the 'correct' winnings and returned to the pub. The bookie, unhappy with this outcome, decided to cash in his insurance policy and phoned Thompson, who arrived shortly afterwards. The argument may have been over a handful of small change but one of Thompson's paying customers had been slighted, which in turn slighted Thompson. From that moment, there was no way back for either faction. By this time, Goldie and Welsh had left the pub and were heading back to Blackhill in Goldie's van. Thompson immediately gave chase in his far more powerful vehicle. The double killing at the railway bridge happened shortly afterwards.

We had an explosive situation on our hands.

A Detective Chief Inspector, now deceased, was called out and I was less than chuffed when I learned that he was extremely wary of Thompson. He seemed to be horrified at the thought of leading this investigation. I encountered many senior police officers like him, who seemed to be afraid of dealing with Arthur Thompson and his brood.

Throughout his criminal career, Thompson was represented by the famous solicitor Joe Beltrami. I have read how clever Beltrami supposedly was in having the charge in relation to this double death reduced from murder to culpable homicide. The truth is that Thompson was never charged with murder. On the night of the incident, the Detective Chief Inspector phoned the senior Procurator Fiscal and pleaded with him that the charge should be one of culpable homicide. This turn of events was less than inspiring to the two keen young officers who had witnessed a double murder! Nevertheless, Arthur was arrested and locked up, and I put the incident to the back of my mind.

Two weeks later, I was phoned at home by a detective who told me that Thompson, now out on bail, was threatening to blow up both my house and John's – Thompson's nickname was 'Bomber Thompson', because he was known to have blown up a pub and social club, businesses whose owners had resisted his efforts to take them over. This was the first time he had threatened to 'do' the homes of police officers.

The response by our bosses was to have our houses guarded, by plain-clothes officers in my case and by the Glasgow Flying Squad in John's. We knew these officers were unlikely to be experienced in dealing with a ruthless gangster like Thompson. Despite the death threats, none of our bosses came out to see either of us that night. Our safety was left to our own devices and a handful of cops.

I was living in a police flat in Springburn Road with my first wife Rena and our daughter Laura, who was only about three years old. In addition, my mother and father were visiting. I thought the best thing to do was to clear the house and get my family to safety. I called a taxi and everyone except me left for my parents' home.

I remained in the flat on my own and began to think of the best strategy to protect myself. I got hold of a large axe and my police baton, then waited to see what would happen. In those days, I was afraid of no one. As I sat there alone, my overwhelming emotion was one of rage. This cheap crook had had the audacity to threaten not just me but also my family and my home! If Thompson or any of his cronies had come anywhere near me that night, I was fully prepared to take them on. I watched every car that passed and scrutinised any that drew up outside the building. However, dawn broke without incident and I called in the plainers, who had been sitting outside in a car. We all had a full Scottish breakfast to complete the night.

John lived in Simshill on the other side of the city. As it happened, he and his wife were out with neighbours on the evening in question, and since the Flying Squad officers guarding his house did not know him personally, they had obtained a photograph of him from the personnel files. In the early hours, a car drew up and a man got out. The detectives immediately approached him and asked, 'Jackson?' He replied automatically, 'Yes,' but as he turned to face them they could see that he did not fit the photograph. He immediately received some summary justice – a severe right-hander to the jaw – before he was tossed onto the bonnet of his car and none too gently searched. At this point it was established that John was sitting, rather the worse for wear, in the back seat of the car. His poor neighbour, who had been driving, was lucky to escape with his testicles intact.

The following day, a Sunday, John and I were told to go to Maitland Street to see my boss, who was extremely angry with us and annoyed at the problems the case was giving him. He told us that he had been instructed by Tom Goodall to bring in Arthur Thompson regarding the threats.

We were told to wait. In strolled Thompson, who was welcomed by the DCI like a long-lost friend and ushered into his office. About ten minutes later, both men emerged and the DCI had the temerity to say to us that he had the assurance of Arthur, as he called him, that our homes and families would be safe from attack as far as he was concerned. At this, John and I, who were both furious at the way we were being treated, faced Thompson in the small room. John stood almost toe-to-toe with him and said, 'Let me tell you something, Thompson – if you come within three miles of my house, or of my brother's house, or of any house belonging to any of our family, you can forget about us being police officers, I'll cut your fucking head off!'

Thompson said nothing but I am sure that he knew it was sincerely meant.

Once Thompson had left the office, the DCI turned on John and said, 'There was no need to speak to him in that manner, Jackson.'

John retorted, 'If you'd had the balls to say it to him, then I wouldn't have needed to.'

At that moment, I could see my career as a CID officer disappearing but the Chief Inspector never said another word about the incident to me.

While Thompson was out on bail awaiting this trial, he changed his vehicle and was now driving a brown and cream MG Magnette, which he always parked outside his house – known as 'The Ponderosa', from the TV series *Bonanza*, because of the rather grotesque brickwork that framed the building. A creature of habit, he tended to leave the house in Provanmill Road between 9 a.m. and noon to go about his business.

One morning, his mother-in-law, Margaret Johnstone, who had been staying overnight, accepted the offer of a lift from him back to her house in Blackhill. Thompson's usual route was to go to the junction with Cumbernauld Road and turn right at the traffic lights to head into town. On this occasion, however, he did a U-turn to head towards Blackhill and, as he did so, he flicked the indicator to flag up his change of direction. He had no inkling that the previous night, while his car had been sitting outside his house, some rascal had surreptitiously crawled under it and attached several sticks of dynamite to the manifold that ran from the engine underneath the front passenger seat. The moment the indicator was switched on, the device was detonated and there was a massive explosion that blew out many of the windows in the street.

Thompson led a charmed life. He survived every assassination attempt. His mother-in-law took the full force of the blast and was killed outright. Thompson was thrown clear and suffered only an injury to his left leg as the gear stick, which was blown from its moorings and through the roof of the car, struck him on the way. Three of the Welsh family, George, Martin and Henry, were indicted for murder and attempted murder.

In what were some of the most dramatic scenes in the history of the old High Court building in the Saltmarket, both Thompson and the Welsh clan stood trial at the same time, with Thompson appearing first in the dock in the north court and then as a witness in the south court against his rivals. Despite the high-profile nature of these trials, security at the building was no greater than usual. It is only in comparatively recent years that threat levels have seen security measures stepped up.

It was early November 1966 and, naturally, John and I gave evidence at Thompson's trial. Nicholas Fairbairn QC, who often worked with Joe Beltrami, defended Thompson. As usual, I was vigorously cross-examined. Fairbairn attacked me over my actions on the night of the incident asking why, having just witnessed a double murder, I did not follow my first duty as a police officer and arrest Thompson at the petrol station. I answered that it was an officer's first duty to protect life. I didn't know at that stage whether the van would explode, as there was petrol all over the road, and, with bus passengers and bystanders milling about, I wanted to use the petrol station's phone to alert the emergency services. Anyway, as I pointed out, I knew where I could find Thompson. In his summing up, Fairbairn tried to dismiss the testimony given by John and me by saying that listening to one Jackson brother was like listening to two as we were so alike and therefore could not corroborate each other!

To my mind, this was an outrageous, not to say curious, statement to make. We both saw the same thing, so of course our testimony was almost identical.

After I gave my evidence, I sat in the public benches to hear the rest of the trial. As I awaited the verdict, DCS Tom Goodall sat beside me. He had shown a tremendous interest in the case and his being seen beside me I took as a great honour and also a sign that I was recognised as a 'proper' detective. In the end, Thompson received a not-proven verdict. He certainly had a top legal team in Beltrami and Fairbairn but I believe to this day that his gang intimidated witnesses to ensure he walked free.

As soon as he was free, Thompson appeared as a witness in the south court. There he did his usual and refused to cooperate with the authorities by failing to speak up against the Welsh brothers. The case was dropped by the Crown and they too walked free from the court.

After we had given evidence, John and I had to be escorted from the building because information had been received that should Thompson be convicted, we were in danger of being shot as we left.

Unbelievably, Thompson had the temerity to apply to the Criminal Injuries Compensation Board for compensation for the injuries he suffered in the car bomb. Likewise, the Welsh family applied for compensation for various incidents. By early 1968, members of the Welsh family had received £1,400 arising purely from incidents involving Thompson.

Soon after the trial, John and his family emigrated to Canada. He stated to the press that the not-proven verdict was one of his reasons for leaving. John was not frightened of any criminal but he was certainly fed up with the gangsters here and the lack of backing the police received from the courts. Coupled with this, he'd been growing disgruntled with life in Scotland generally and he and his wife decided that they could offer their four children a better life in Canada. Accordingly, he had applied for and had been accepted by the Metropolitan Toronto Police.

John made a success of his new life, rising to the rank of inspector and sub-divisional officer, although he continued to be a tearaway and was feared by both bandits and police alike. He was famed not only for his ruthlessness but also because he could waggle his ears at will. Once, during a trial, the accused stood up in court and complained to the judge that John was waggling his ears at him, presumably in a threatening manner. The claim was dismissed and the man was duly locked up. Later, at an official function, the judge asked John's opinion of the ned's behaviour in court. John merely waggled his ears in reply. The judge almost choked on his drink.

John led a colourful, eventful and fruitful life. He was a good friend to me and to my third wife, Katie, and gave us support through a very stressful time of our lives. You could always depend on him to give you a lift when you were down. When he was stricken with throat cancer, he contacted us and asked us to go over to Canada and spend some time with him before he went into hospital. We agreed immediately and stayed with him until he went in for the operation. We remained in Canada until we knew he had undergone the operation and was recovering and then flew home that night. When we arrived at the house, there was a message to phone Canada. While we were somewhere over the Atlantic, my wild brother John had taken a turn for the worse and died.

He was only 58 and had never smoked in his life.

Due to our respective professions, Arthur Thompson and I often crossed paths. The next main occasion was about 20 years later while I was in charge of the Serious Crime Squad. By this time, Thompson had a family and his eldest son, 'young Arthur', had tried to emulate his gangster father but had been ripped off in a drug deal in which he had paid £30,000 for a load of gear that proved not to be the high-class merchandise he had been expecting. An established older criminal of Irish origin who had graced the Glasgow crime scene for many years carried out this scam. The Irishman certainly would not have tried this move on old Arthur but the general feeling among the criminal fraternity was that young Arthur was a bit of a pillock and was seen as easier pickings.

When he realised that he had been done over, he went bleating to his dad, whose reaction was to send his heavy team, led by a young and violent associate, to have a strong word with the Irishman. This did not have the desired effect, as the Irish gangster was a pretty rough customer himself and he refused to return the cash. This little deal had come to the ears of some of my officers in the Serious Crime Squad, who in turn informed me. The calibre of individuals involved on either side was not such that they would come crying to the police for assistance. They would want to sort it out among themselves. It was only a matter of time before things flared up. What happened took everyone by surprise. The Irishman had friends across the water who were associated with the IRA. He called on one of these friends, a hit man who ran a training camp for up-and-coming young thugs, to come to Scotland and lend a hand by assassinating Thompson senior.

Thompson was at that time running a demolition business from a yard in Carmyle on the outskirts of the East End of Glasgow. His brother-in-law, quite a decent, hard-working chap, had previously owned the yard until Thompson made him an offer he could not refuse. He was kept on the payroll after the takeover. No doubt his genuine expertise was needed.

Thompson set up an office on site in a static caravan. One morning, when he was ensconced in that office, with several of his men working in the yard and his brother-in-law just outside the caravan, a tall, bearded man entered the premises and asked in a broad Irish accent if Mr Thompson was available. The brother-in-law, perhaps naively, directed this man to the caravan, followed him in and stood just inside the door.

Thompson was sitting behind his desk at the far end of the office. The man walked calmly towards him. Without a word, he proceeded to pull out an extremely large handgun from inside his jacket, pointed it directly at Thompson and, without further ado, pulled the trigger. Later, Thompson's brother-in-law said that the gun was so large it just seemed to keep 'coming and coming'.

Thompson's guardian angels were working overtime that day. Believe it or not, the gun misfired, giving him time to leap over the desk at the gunman, who immediately ran for the door. Thompson arrived at the door just as the gunman turned back and opened fire again. This time, the weapon functioned properly and bullets flew everywhere. The workers in the yard began to bombard the gunman with all manner of missiles. Dodging the barrage, the would-be assassin ran out of the premises, jumped into a waiting car and escaped.

Meanwhile, Thompson discovered he'd been shot in the groin by a bullet that had apparently ricocheted off the cobbles. Instead of heading for the closest hospital, however, the bold Arthur headed for the Nuffield MacAlpine private hospital in the West End of the city. He told the unsuspecting surgeons who examined and then operated on him that he had suffered his injury when a piece of metal sheared off from a metal lathe. Thompson had gone to the private hospital hoping that the incident would not be reported. The surgeons were, of course, highly experienced and knew a bullet when they saw one. They duly notified the police. By the time senior officers arrived at the hospital, Thompson was in a private room being guarded by his favourite lawyer, who had obviously been summoned post-haste. Unsurprisingly, Thompson told the police nothing. Joe Beltrami remained present throughout the interview at his request – perhaps not the normal action of a victim in a criminal shooting, but Thompson apparently considered Joe Beltrami as more of a friend than just his lawyer. I do not know if that feeling was reciprocated. Two days after being shot, Thompson signed himself out of hospital, either to protect his hard-man image by letting everyone know that he was alive and well, or because he didn't like the price of the private medical treatment. Big Arthur was known to be thrifty.

The inquiry into the shooting was conducted by officers from London Road Police Office in the East End of the city, where the yard was located. Of course, my squad was most interested in developments and we were actively seeking to identify and track down this apparently unknown assassin. An excellent officer in the squad, Detective Inspector Eddie Ellington, soon came up with the information that the gunman had been brought from Ireland specifically to do the shooting. Eddie also learned that the gunman was staying in Cathcart Road, just south of Hampden Park. I phoned the detective superintendent in charge of Eastern Division rather late on a Friday night to alert him as to what was happening and the information we had received. At this point, he seemed quite happy to let my squad deal with it.

I then contacted the duty Procurator Fiscal, Len Higson, with whom I'd had many previous dealings and whom I'd found to be a very sharp and intelligent gentleman. I requested a warrant for the house where the gunman was staying, expecting the response from Len to be that he would contact a sheriff. However, he totally surprised me by saying that this would not be necessary as he had it within his power to grant a warrant on the strength of the reliable information I had supplied over the phone. Not only that, but we could enter the house without being in physical possession of the document. This was a first. Previously in my experience it had always been necessary for the fiscal to contact a sheriff for the warrant to be sworn out in front of him. I was delighted with the fiscal's swift and positive response.

My officers went to the house early in the morning and burst in to find the suspect, who matched the description given by Thompson's brother-in-law, still in bed. He went with the officers without causing any trouble. The house had been under close surveillance, so we were pretty certain he would be inside and that there were no nasty shocks in store. Even so, every precaution had been taken, including arming my men. The house was searched but no guns were found. This was not a surprise, as a professional hit man would not retain a gun used in a crime and would dispose of it shortly after any shooting. If the Clyde could be completely drained, it would be an armourer's wet dream. The bottom of the river must be covered with such weapons.

The suspect was taken to the Central Police Office at Stewart Street for an identification parade that afternoon, with the witnesses being Thompson, his unfortunate brother-in-law and the other workers from the yard. All told, some seven witnesses viewed the parade. I did not expect Thompson to identify the suspect and was not proved wrong, but I was hopeful that some of the other witnesses might. They did not. As the witnesses refused to identify the suspect and more or less retracted their original statements – again clearly after having been instructed to do so by Thompson – no further action could be taken. It was blatantly obvious that they were obeying instructions from their boss not to cooperate with the police inquiry. The gangster was always the same when dealing with the police. Even when, many years later, his own son was murdered outside his front door, he forbade his family to give true statements.

The following morning, I received a summons to attend a meeting with the Detective Chief Superintendent who was the head of CID. He was upset regarding the events of the previous day, despite having agreed that the Serious Crime Squad would take the inquiry forward. One remark made to me during our heated discussion was that by parading this hired IRA killer in front of Thompson I had put the suspect's life in danger. That the hit man being placed in jeopardy should bother me or any other officer was beyond my comprehension. This gunman, after all, had attempted to murder someone, even if the intended victim was a hardened crook. I really had no worries as to what was liable to happen to him. This was another example of an officer being wary of dealing with Thompson.

With witnesses refusing to identify the suspect, the case was very much dead in the water. There was, however, one last scene to play out. When arresting the man in Cathcart Road, my officers had routinely taken possession of his belongings, including £300 in cash. Following normal procedure, this was kept in a safe at police headquarters. If the case had gone to trial, this money would have been lodged as evidence, probably as proof of partial payment for the shooting of Thompson, depending on what his life was deemed to be worth.

About a week after the shooting, I was in my office at police headquarters when I received a phone call from the commissionaire saying that there was a large, bearded Irishman at the main entrance who wished to have a word with me regarding his possessions. I asked for the visitor to be sent to my office and awaited his arrival with great interest. I had not had the opportunity to speak with him at the time of his arrest and I wanted to assess this man. To my mind, he was obviously very dangerous but was either downright stupid or extremely brave to walk into the offices of the Serious Crime Squad on his own.

He turned out to be an amiable individual, who stood to attention in front of my desk as a soldier would. I asked him if he was heading back to Ireland immediately – this would seem to be a sensible course of action in the light of what had taken place. He said that he would be staying in Glasgow for a while as he was enjoying the attention he was receiving in the saunas owned by another Irishman. Although I tried, there proved to be no point in speaking to him regarding the Thompson incident. He just clammed up. I handed him his possessions, including the money. I also gave him one piece of advice – if he was going to have another crack at Thompson, he should spend the money on a better gun. The weapon used in the assassination attempt had been identified as a First World War long-barrelled Colt revolver and was obviously not up to the job.

The man remained in Glasgow for several months but there was no attempt to exact revenge. At least, nothing that came to the notice of the police. This suggests that Thompson was becoming more forgiving or more easily frightened: either being highly unlikely. Perhaps not even Arthur Thompson was crazy enough to take on the IRA.

During the period when I was a detective superintendent in charge of the Strathclyde Serious Crime Squad, a post I held from 1985 to 1987, I had the pleasure of working with many excellent detectives. One in particular was Sergeant Willie Wylie – for obvious reasons, his nickname was Wily Willie. He was about 6 ft 2 in. tall, with a rugby-player build, strawberry-blond hair and glasses. He was once described to me as looking like a blond Clark Kent. This caused great hilarity in the team.

Willie was nobody's fool. He approached me one day, about a year after the shooting incident, to say that he had received information regarding one of the worst villains who lived in the Easterhouse area of Glasgow. This man was Jonah McKenzie, also known as 'Cyclops' because he had lost an eye in a gang fight. This nickname changed to Blind Jonah when he had his other eye taken out in another fight.

Jonah, it seemed, was dealing heroin from his ground-floor flat in Easterhouse. His style was to issue the smack from a window to punters who arrived in the back court. Willie asked me if he could set up an observation post nearby to study the comings and goings at the front and rear of Jonah's house. I agreed to this and assigned a team of detectives to work with him.

Almost immediately, things began to happen. On the first day, deals were being done at the back of the house, with a steady stream of customers being seen there. At the same time, a car appeared at the front of the close. Officers identified one of the car's two occupants as being young Arthur Thompson, known as 'Fatboy' and also as 'The Mars Bar Kid' – in prison, where he was afraid that other prisoners would tamper with his food because of their hatred for his father, he had an almost constant supply of the chocolate bars on hand.

Knowing his connection with high-level crime and the drug trade, detectives immediately closed in on him. Young Arthur and his pal panicked and the car took off at a great rate of knots. Police cars in the vicinity gave pursuit and during the chase Thompson was seen to lob a number of small packages from the car windows. The car was eventually stopped and he and his accomplice were arrested. The packages were recovered along the route; they contained a large quantity of heroin.

While this was happening, the officers who were still at Jonah's house decided to move in to prevent destruction of evidence. The easiest access to the flat was through the kitchen window from which Jonah had been dealing. Although it was on the ground floor, it was relatively high up and so our very own Superman heaved one of his smaller compatriots up through the open window. Jonah was still in the kitchen with some of the drugs and was knocked breathless when the small detective landed on top of him. The swift action taken prevented any drugs being disposed of and a search turned up a considerable cache of heroin elsewhere in the house.

Clearly, getting young Arthur under these circumstances was a major bonus, as the target had initially been Jonah McKenzie, a known crook but still relatively small-time. Arthur was further up the chain of supply.

The arrested criminals were all taken to Shettleston Police Office in Chester Street and I decided to pay a visit. Young Arthur was certainly not a chip off the old block. He would talk quite willingly to police officers and even fire in his accomplices in an attempt to save his own skin. He traded very much on his father's reputation and was, not to put too fine a point on it, a shitebag.

I had never spoken to him before. I introduced myself to him in his cell.

'Are you the boss?' he asked.

'I'm in charge of the Serious Crime Squad.'

He nodded, this obviously meeting with his approval. 'Can you help me out here?'

'We'll do what we can for you, Arthur,' I said, having no intention of doing anything of the sort, 'but you've got to help us. You've got to give us something in return.'

He fell silent as he thought about this. Then he nodded. He'd see what he could do. I knew he would.

Before I left I said, 'I know your dad, by the way. Tell him Joe Jackson says hello.'

I often allowed myself a wry smile when I envisaged his father's reaction to young Arthur confidently telling him that Joe Jackson was looking after him.

In 1985, Arthur Thompson junior received a sentence of 12 years for drug dealing and it was towards the completion of this sentence, in August 1991, while on a home visit, that he was shot dead outside his father's home. Six bullets were fired and three found their mark. One grazed his cheek, another smashed ribs, a third entered through his back and eventually found his heart. The first and third slugs – to the head and the back – were reminiscent of his father's style of execution. A former Thompson enforcer, Paul Ferris, was charged with the murder but cleared at the High Court in June 1992.

Apart from this indirect contact, I had no further dealings with Arthur Thompson. He was, without a doubt, the most powerful crook in the north side of Glasgow and his tentacles reached out far beyond the city. He was, however, not the 'Godfather of Glasgow', as has been claimed. There were others, equally active, equally vicious, who did not receive the same press coverage. Thompson senior died from a heart attack in his home in 1993, a broken man who never recovered from the death of his oldest son and a far cry from the violent villain who had threatened to murder my brother and me.

I can't say I mourned his passing.

four

Dying to Dance

During 1968 and 1969, three specific murders took place in Glasgow, all of young women who had been at the Barrowland dance hall in the Gallowgate on the evening prior to meeting their deaths. Two of them had attended the ballroom on the Thursday 'Over 25s' night, when married men and women often turned up without their spouses. It was unkindly known as 'grab a granny night'.

The first victim was 25-year-old Patricia Docker, an attractive, dark-haired nurse at the nearby Victoria Infirmary. Separated from her soldier husband, she and her four-year-old son lived with her parents in Langside Place, a quiet residential street in the Battlefield area in Glasgow's south side. One night in February 1968, she told her parents that she was going out to the dancing at the Majestic at the top of Hope Street in the city centre. Known to cops as the Magic Stick, this was a slightly more upmarket dance hall than the Barrowland. When she had not returned home by the following morning, her parents reported her missing. What they did not know was that a young woman's naked body had already been found in a service lane near to where they lived. It was, of course, their daughter.

I was working as a detective constable in Maitland Street when the call went out for all city divisions to supply two detectives to report to the murder caravan, which had been set up by officers from the Southern Division at the lane. On their arrival, the detectives were met by Detective Chief Superintendent Tom Goodall, head of Glasgow CID, along with a senior detective from Craigie Street, the divisional headquarters. It was a typical Glasgow suburban alleyway – a narrow passageway with insets on either side for residents to store their dustbins, and tall wooden doors set into the garden walls. In those days, it was not appreciated how important it was to preserve the locus in as pristine a condition as possible, so all the flatfoots were allowed to go into this lane and view the body. In the later part of my career as a senior detective, I would always allow my detectives to view the crime scene – but only after it had been thoroughly forensically examined and photographed, and the body removed.

A door-to-door canvass of the houses surrounding the lane was conducted and officers were amazed to learn how many of the householders had been somewhere they shouldn't have on the night in question. I understand quite a few divorces ensued. Inquiries were also made at the Majestic. It was some days before we learned that Patricia had, in fact, gone to the Barrowland instead. This led to the first bum steer: a nutcase who had been at the Majestic insisted that he had danced with the murdered woman. His claim was quickly disproved but centring our investigation on the Majestic lost us valuable time. There was also a line of inquiry surrounding a vague suggestion that a white car had been seen in the vicinity. Meanwhile, frogmen searched the nearby River Cart for clothing and personal items that were not found near the body.

During the course of this murder inquiry, which lasted initially for two weeks, the team of detectives worked fourteen-hour days from 8 a.m. until 10 p.m. Each morning, we had to report to the murder caravan to be allocated our tasks for that day. One morning, we arrived and the caravan had gone. Immediately, my thought – and that of every other detective – was that the crime had been solved while we were off duty. This was not the case; it was just that the resources were needed in Cardonald, where two pensioners had been brutally killed in their high-rise home. This part of Glasgow was covered by the Govan Station, which was already investigating a murder and rape on a railway line near to Paisley Road West. As a result, all detectives from other divisions who had been working on the Patricia Docker murder were redirected to Govan to assist. The local divisional guys at Craigie Street were left to get on with the Patricia Docker investigation. Incidentally, one man, who was snared through fingerprint evidence, committed all three of these Govan murders. A fruit shop owner with premises near Govan Road, he was ultimately classed by the head psychiatrist at Carstairs State Mental Hospital as psychopathic.

Despite the efforts of the local detectives, the Patricia Docker case remained unsolved. As is the nature of police work, other cases became more pressing, although the inquiry would never really be closed. The dead woman's name duly faded from the pages of newspapers and the minds of the public at large. Only her loved ones remembered and mourned her. What no one knew at the time was that this bright, vivacious young woman's name was to become forever linked with a series of murders that haunt Glasgow to this day.

In August 1969, another partially clothed body was found, this time in a derelict tenement in MacKeith Street in Bridgeton. This turned out to be unmarried mother of three Jemima 'Mima' McDonald – and she too had last been seen alive at the Barrowland Ballroom. Once again, it was visited by police officers, including DCS Goodall, who asked patrons if they had been in the dance hall the night Mima was last seen. Had they seen her? Did they see who was with her? Did they see who she left with? They gleaned enough information to draw up an identikit picture of the man last soon with the victim and this image was released to the press – the first time such a step had been taken in a Scottish murder probe. DCS Goodall knew this might prove problematic with regard to identification if the case came to court but this bid to attract more witnesses was a calculated risk. Nevertheless, the trail ran cold. The murder of Jemima McDonald, so similar to that of Patricia Docker although the two were not as yet officially linked, remained unsolved. I was not involved in this inquiry and I continued to work as normal in the Northern Division. However, that was about to change.

In October 1969, just over two months after Jemima McDonald was killed, another woman was found murdered, this time at the rear of a common close in Earl Street, Scotstoun. Again the body was partially clothed, again the victim had attended the Barrowland Ballroom. This time, though, police had a witness. The dead woman was 29-year-old Helen Puttock, who had gone out for the evening with her sister Jean Langford. Helen had left the dance hall in a taxi with Jean and two men, both of whom were allegedly called John. One of them said he came from Castlemilk and was Jean's 'lumber'. He got out of the taxi near Glasgow Cross, leaving Helen, Jean and the other man in the vehicle. Despite frequent appeals, 'Castlemilk John' never came forward. Perhaps if he had, the case would not be the mystery it is today.

The trio within the taxi continued to the west side of the city. Apparently, during the course of the journey, the man provided some relatively precise biographical details, although how many of them were true only he knows. He also made references to parts of the Bible. This fact was released to the press and some very smart reporter labelled him 'Bible John'. The name has stuck.

Jean was dropped off first, leaving Helen and the man alone in the taxi. It was only a short jaunt to Scotstoun and what happened next is open to conjecture. The following morning, Helen was found strangled about three closes away from her own home. That made three women in eighteen months who had attended the Barrowland and had later been found raped and strangled. Some top CID officers believed that there was definitely a link. The man at the head of CID was now DCS Elphinstone Dalgleish, who took over when Tom Goodall died suddenly in October 1969. His sad death was a bitter blow to many officers who had worked for him over the years.

The officer in charge of the so-called 'Bible John inquiry' was Detective Superintendent Joe Beattie. I first met him when I was in plain clothes in Northern Division, when, along with Davy Frew, I was attached to the CID for every second night shift. Joe was a detective sergeant on this shift, partnered with a DC called Tom MacDonald. From them I learned a great deal about interview techniques and the different styles that could be adopted, depending on who you were questioning. Joe had been born and brought up in the Garscube Road area and later worked there as a cop. He was well known in police circles for having a great many touts in the area. They were called 'Joe's half-crown touts', as this was their normal payment for the information. I don't think the equivalent 12 pence nowadays would cut much ice. On day shift, Joe had a colleague named Jimmy McInnes. They were to the CID what Davy Frew and I were to the uniformed branch in that they were forever locking up good criminals.

I next met up with him when I was at Maitland Street CID and he was promoted in as Detective Chief Inspector. As a DS, he was always smiling and joking but now he seemed to take himself very seriously. By the time of the Bible John case, he liked to be known as 'Mr Beattie'. He worked almost round the clock in trying to catch this killer, or killers, and I have no doubt he was totally obsessed. His second-in-command was a great boss called 'Yorkie' Lloyd who, believe it or not, came from Yorkshire, almost making him a foreigner in those days. Neither of these men received much help from other senior officers at headquarters, presumably because they had nothing to contribute by way of investigatory skills.

The 'Bible John headquarters' was in Partick Police Office, known to cops as 'The Marine'. This was the station that covered the Scotstoun area, where Helen Puttock had lived and died. Around January 1970, after this third inquiry had been running for three months, it was decided to bring in some fresh detectives, as many of the people working on the case had been putting in fourteen-hour days and had had no time off. I was one of the detectives who were brought in at this point, when the inquiry was, to be honest, going stale. I would spend a year on the hunt. We were given certain directions regarding the man we were seeking.

One of the lines of inquiry involved visiting dentists throughout the Glasgow area; Jean Langford had said that there was a slight deformity in the suspect's front teeth, inasmuch as the right slightly crossed over the left. The fourth upper right tooth was also missing. I spoke to many dentists about this. While they could understand that the front teeth would perhaps be noticeable, they all said that it would be extremely difficult to notice that the fourth upper right tooth was missing, other than through a proper dental examination. It would appear that Jean had been able to spot this in the back of a darkened taxi. She was the first to admit that she'd had a couple of drinks before going to the dancing that night. However, Jean tried her level best to help catch her sister's murderer and spent many, many hours with detectives going to the various dance halls throughout Glasgow in an attempt to spot him. I feel that she was, as you would expect, put under immense pressure to come up with as detailed a description of the suspect as was humanly possible. It has to be said that her description, on which the subsequent photofits and famed artist's impression were based, was not weighed against the statements of other people. Barrowland bouncers, for instance, had a discussion with the suspect while he was at a cigarette machine in the foyer. I don't know why their rather different description was summarily discounted.

Going into an inquiry after several months have passed makes it hard to pick up the various threads. Sometimes, I had the feeling that we were simply going through the motions because of the strength of character of the person leading the inquiry. Sometimes, though, an officer would produce what would be considered as a more than reasonable suspect, but he would be dismissed by a shake of Mr Beattie's head. This was most discouraging for all of the team.

We were sometimes asked to perform some unconventional duties. For instance, I formed part of what the press called the 'Marine Formation Dance Team'. This was a team of detectives assigned to attend city dance halls, including the Barrowland, the Magic Stick and the Plaza. Our brief was to dance with customers and question them, while showing off some nifty footwork. Even the ugly detectives proved popular dance partners, as the ladies felt safe with them. It was a dirty job but someone had to do it. I learned a pretty mean samba through being involved in this aspect of the investigation.

On another occasion, I was asked to collect a man from Lennoxtown and take him to Partick Police Office, where Joe and Jean were waiting. This chap claimed to be a medium. He said that he'd had a vision that Bible John was staying in the Birmingham area in a flat above a shop with a woman who had a young child. He told me this story as I drove him to the police office. Quite honestly, I did not know why we were wasting our time on such a wild goose chase. He went into the office, where he was interviewed by Mr Beattie in Jean's presence. This meeting ended acrimoniously, with the medium hurtling out through the door, his feet never touching the ground. A colleague and I had to dust him down and give him a cup of tea before returning him to Lennoxtown.

That was not the only brush with the supernatural. Dutch psychic Gerard Croiset became involved in the case while he was in Scotland at the request of the *Daily Record* to investigate the disappearance of a young woman in Dumfries and Galloway. The information he provided, regarding a street in Govan, revealed very little. Croiset was 'handled' by the three senior officers in the inquiry – Joe Beattie, DS Tommy Valentine and DCI 'Yorkie' Lloyd. Personally, I've never had much time for all that psychic malarkey. I've always thought that dealing with such off-the-wall characters has nothing to do with proper detective work. Joe Beattie was undoubtedly totally dedicated to achieving a proper result but he reached a point where he was grasping at straws. I felt that he was too narrowly focused in the way in which he was dealing with the inquiry. However, I did learn from this and made sure in later years, when running major inquiries, that I listened to the views of all the detectives and incident room staff to make sure that I covered not just one angle but all angles. I have found that this is the proper way to deal with major investigations, because you can be totally focused on one suspect when another one will be unearthed through the hard work of good young detectives. This kind of lead should never be discounted. The views of the younger members of a squad should be examined, even if occasionally they seem fatuous. Sometimes, young people have a clearer view and this should not be ignored.

It is my belief that too much information was issued to the press in this case, including the nugget that the suspect quoted the Bible. The press is a valuable tool in a murder probe but the release of too much information can help suspects cover their tracks. Reporters were even told about the dance hall squads. Certainly, the 'Marine Formation Dance Team' was a bit of light relief from the rigours of normal detective work but it also had a serious function. By alerting the press we also alerted the killer, so there really was no hope of him turning up at the dance halls.

Despite the descriptions, despite the witnesses, despite the identikits and photofits and oil paintings, despite thousands of man-hours, despite the acres of press coverage, no one has been charged with these three killings. I would never discount the efforts of Joe Beattie. Good cop though he was, in this case at least he was blinkered and would not accept views that differed from his own. He passed on a few years ago having suffered severe illness later in his life. I met him at a police function after he had retired and I am glad to say that, although not in the best of health, the smiling and joking Joe had reappeared.

I believe these murders should have been separated and dealt with by different senior investigating officers, or SIOs, who could then have compared results. This would have ensured that any perceived link was genuine and not created by one man's obsession or by press hysteria. We can speculate on how many killers there were but the fact that they were investigated from the outset of the Helen Puttock case as one left no room for manoeuvre. Any investigation needs to be viewed dispassionately and not coloured by the judgement of any single person, whatever his rank may be.

As for Bible John, if such a multiple killer ever existed, he has slipped almost into legend. He became a sort of bogeyman whose spectre would appear whenever there was an unsolved killing of a woman in Glasgow. There have been books, articles, documentaries and even a comic book about him. A few years ago, DNA technology was used to link a one-time suspect – John McInnes – with the death of Helen Puttock. A semen stain had been found on the dead woman's tights and there was also a bite mark; with the development of genetic fingerprinting it was thought that a match could be found among the hundreds of suspects.

The failure of the exercise does not surprise me. Physical evidence like stained clothing was very poorly stored and preserved at the time of the inquiry. For instance, bloodstained clothing used to be stored in plastic bags, which caused them to ferment eventually. Scientists told us to dry them out and put them in paper bags. The drying-out process usually involved the items being draped over pipes in the boiler room of police offices. I cannot say for certain how the tights in this case were stored but I cannot see them being treated as gingerly as would be necessary for a clear DNA comparison. However, it was felt that there was a close enough match between it and the DNA samples given voluntarily by relatives of the suspect to merit the exhumation of John McInnes's body. I would have had to have been 100 per cent certain that he was my man before taking that step. DNA is a great tool in police work – but that's all it is. It should not take the place of proper detective work. The investigation was much publicised but ultimately failed to lay the ghost to rest – no clear DNA match was found and even the comparison of the bite mark and his teeth was inconclusive.

ARMED ROBBERS

After 15 years' service, I was promoted to detective sergeant and posted to the Eastern Division working out of the old Tobago Street office. There, my colleagues were good police officers, some of whom went on to achieve very high ranks.

While at the East, I was involved in arresting a gunman who was responsible for a series of bank raids and other robberies throughout Glasgow. This man was a Fagin-type character inasmuch as when he held up the banks he used two young teenagers, actually issuing them with guns before they committed the crimes.

One night when I was working late shift, a report came in from an old-age pensioner who stayed alone in high flats in Garvald Street that three people had arrived at his door carrying firearms and had threatened him. The man slammed the door in their faces and shouted at the top of his voice for help from anyone who could hear. He also phoned the police. This scared off the three at the door. It would appear that these young hoodlums knew that he stayed on his own and might well have been having a bit of practice with the guns and their terrifying effect.

The uniforms who responded reported back to the duty officer, who in turn contacted the senior CID man on duty, who happened to be me. As the three were still believed to be in the high flats and known to be armed, it was agreed that I should be issued with a firearm before I attended the locus. The only officers trained in firearms then were some CID officers. Training was very basic, consisting of a two-day session twice a year at the firing range at the Glasgow Police Training Centre in Oxford Street in the Gorbals. There we were given a handgun – a Smith & Wesson revolver – and ordered to blast merry hell out of targets. This training had only recently been introduced for divisional detectives and they each had to qualify before they could be sent out into the streets armed.

The Garvald Street incident was the first time I had been issued with firearms in a 'live' situation and I got the shock of my life when I was handed what looked like a First World War Colt revolver in a military canvas holster with a whistle attached. It had obviously been kept in the duty officer's safe at the bar in Tobago Street since time immemorial. In fact, I thought I could make out Buffalo Bill's fingerprints on it. This was a far cry from the cinema hero then in vogue, Dirty Harry. What I had been given was far from being the most powerful handgun in the world.

Apart from being somewhat flippant regarding the firearm I received, I was not really ready to take on this responsibility, as I felt that my training had been less than adequate. Shooting at cardboard targets was one thing; it was quite another to be faced with the possibility of drawing and aiming at a living, breathing human being. Not to mention one who might shoot first. It was with some trepidation that I left the office 'tooled up'.

Incidents involving firearms were virtually unknown, which raised the possibility that the old man was just an attention-seeker. I spoke to him and was convinced that he was telling the truth. However, despite a thorough search of the high flats the three individuals were not found.

The following week, when I was back on day shift, crime information bulletins were issued regarding three armed men committing a series of robberies. The incident I had dealt with the previous week was added to these cases because of the similarities. I learned that the

Serious Crime Squad had identified suspects and that the two youths had been arrested. Their older companion, who was known to carry a sawn-off shotgun and to frequent the city centre, had not been caught yet. Finally, officers from the squad spotted him in Waterloo Street near to Anderston Bus Station (now demolished). They reported that he had his right hand wrapped in a polythene bag.

When the man realised he was under observation, he decided to try to shake the officers off by jumping onto a bus filled with American tourists heading to Prestwick Airport. Not willing to let him get away, the unarmed Serious Crime Squad officers, led by Detective Sergeant Willie Anderson, pursued him onto the bus and tried to grab him before he could harm anyone, but during the struggle he managed to fire the shotgun hidden inside the plastic bag. The blast punched a hole through the front of the bus. Fortunately, no one was injured.

When the target was first spotted, I was on my way with another detective from Tobago Street to police headquarters in Pitt Street. As we drove along the Clydeside, we heard the various calls on the police radio regarding the events in the bus station, culminating in urgent calls for assistance, and we decided to lend a hand. We were there in minutes. We ditched the car and sprinted into the terminus. My neighbour was running ahead of me and had just passed the front of the bus when the shotgun erupted. We both jumped on the bus and assisted in removing the armed man, who was struggling like fury trying to escape. I took possession of the double-barrelled side-by-side shotgun and cracked it open. Smoke drifted from the exposed chambers and I saw that the gunman had only managed to fire one barrel – there was still a live cartridge wedged in the second. If there were cops in Glasgow more relieved than us, I'd be very surprised.

The gunman was, of course, not treated very gently as he was removed from the bus, fighting all the time. In fact, he was pulled in a number of different directions at once by several very irate police officers and received a hefty kick in the knackers, which seemed to calm him down. He was handcuffed then thrown into the back of a police vehicle and taken to Cranstonhill Police Office, where he was charged and locked up. All of the officers involved in the arrest were pretty shocked and as we stood discussing the incident, a Good Samaritan produced a half-bottle of brandy, which he emptied into a large mug for us to share. We each took a drink but it did not have the desired effect, as we were all as high as kites from what had taken place.

The American passengers had come to quaint old Scotland for a pleasant tour of the whisky distilleries. They did not expect to be flying home to an American city quieter than Glasgow. All the police officers involved received high commendations from the Chief Constable for that one. At least two of my colleagues received medals. They were two excellent cops, Willie Anderson and Donald Maule, who were closest to the ned when he fired the shotgun and were the most at risk. Willie Anderson had a very successful career and eventually finished up as the commander of the Scottish Crime Squad. Sadly, Donald passed away a number of years ago.

The Serious Crime Squad

I n 1976, the Glasgow Force and those of surrounding counties were amalgamated to form Strathclyde Police. The Serious Crime Squad had not existed before this but was now made up of detectives from all the various areas, replacing the old Glasgow Flying Squad. Most of them were from the old city divisions but there was a smattering of officers from outside Glasgow. The bosses were John MacDougall and John Blincow, from Glasgow and Lanarkshire respectively. The squad consisted of three teams, each headed by a detective inspector with two detective sergeants and six detective constables.

I only stayed in the Eastern Division for a matter of months before being transferred to the Serious Crime Squad. As a detective sergeant in the squad, there were quite a few scary moments but some rather funny ones as well. For instance, a Govan-based gang, later to be run by an infamous gangster called Walter Norval, had made a name for itself with hold-ups at banks, supermarkets and even a hospital for its payroll. Always armed, this was an extremely dangerous mob. We learned that they were planning to rob the bus depot in Helen Street in Govan on the Friday of the wages delivery. The gang's plan was simple – they were going to ambush the security van staff inside the garage complex, threaten them with guns and steal the cash. The intention was that they would then drive away to a nearby underpass where they would ditch the car, the idea being that if they were pursued they would run through the underpass to make their escape – they apparently had cycles hidden nearby. They were supposedly going to split up and meet later to divvy up the takings.

The flaw in their plan was that the bus garage was situated directly across from the police garage in Helen Street. Although these premises did not have a constant police presence – it was merely where police vehicles were serviced or repaired – they were to prove very handy when the Serious Crime Squad was tipped off about the proposed 'blag'.

It was left to the Detective Chief Inspector, the second-highest rank in the squad, to devise a plan to foil this crime. This man, who is now deceased, decided that he and a team of six detectives should be involved in a stakeout when the wages were to be delivered at around 7 a.m. on the following Friday. It was highly unusual for a senior officer to be present during a 'turn', but this was no usual senior officer. Sometimes, we felt that he was a few pages short of a full crime report, if you know what I mean. He decided that we would all be armed, not an unwise precaution given this gang's 'previous'. Within the Serious Crime Squad, we had our own store of weapons, which consisted only of Smith & Wesson .38 calibre handguns. The snub-nosed, four-inch barrelled guns were generally preferred because they could be carried in an unobtrusive shoulder holster. There were also guns available with six-inch barrels. As we were about to leave the office, the senior officer said that he wanted, as he put it, 'a big gun'. Very John Wayneish, I thought. Or maybe he'd been rehearsing Dirty Harry's 'Do you feel lucky?' speech.

Six of us were to go to the police garage, where we would meet up with four traffic cops, expert drivers who had extremely fast cars parked in readiness behind the main garage door which we could swiftly bundle into should there be a chase. We positioned ourselves at the windows on the first floor. The traffic cops had been fully briefed on their role but were rather taken aback when the DCI removed his jacket to reveal his big gun. The seventh member of the team, Detective Constable Brian Laird, had been placed on the top floor of a stationary double-decker bus inside the garage without the knowledge of the garage staff. Equipped with a radio and in constant contact with us, his brief was to keep watch on the office premises and inform us of the arrival of the security vehicle or sight of the gang.

At one point, Brian's voice dropped and he whispered into the radio that someone had entered the bus and was coming up the stairs. By this time he was lying on the floor under the seats in order not to be spotted. The person who had entered the bus was a member of the cleaning staff and, totally unaware of the cop's presence, he directed a strong jet of hose water along the floor of the upper deck, totally soaking Brian. Brian, being a true professional, did not swear into his radio until the cleaner had left the bus. Then he began spluttering and cursing. Over in the police garage, the rest of us, except the DCI and the rather stunned traffic cops, were also on the floor in fits of laughter.

Things, however, were about to get worse for us. The DCI thought that the windows from where we were taking our observations were too large and obvious. Although we were not hanging out of them, he suggested that some of us should go to a nearby greengrocer's shop and obtain a couple of empty slatted orange boxes. His idea was that we could stand nearer the window with the orange boxes over our heads while looking through the slats – a cunning disguise. The traffic cops thought that we were completely off our heads and were obviously wondering, 'How do these guys get to carry guns?'

We all chose to ignore the suggestion from our glorious leader.

This particular robbery did not take place that day. The following week, we again took observations without the assistance of the DCI, which was a pity as we all turned up armed not only with Smith & Wessons but also with empty orange boxes. In the end, the raid did not go down at all. As sometimes happens, the information we'd received was flawed. Or perhaps the Govan gang had found out about us skulking around nearby fruit shops looking for empty orange boxes.

The ridiculous tone of this incident was a complete exception. I relished the fact that working in the Serious Crime Squad put me right at the cutting edge of police work. The squad took a keen interest in all major crimes as criminals were often starting to carry guns to rob banks as well as be involved in murders and other serious crimes.

I was given a key role – to form a cohort of 'chosen men'. There were not the same opportunities in those days for policewomen – it was only around this time that the policewomen's department was disbanded and the job became 'equal' for males and females. There was a female detective officer in each squad – really good female officers who could sometimes knock the socks off their male counterparts. This specialist team carried firearms as required and I am proud to say that we assisted territorial divisions in many serious cases and also in arresting a great number of gang members responsible for hold-ups and other crimes.

CARSTAIRS MASSACRE

However, there were two men who, although arrested, managed to avoid the form of justice that some of us were quite prepared to dish out. Their crimes were particularly horrific and they had proved themselves quite capable of murdering anyone who got in their way. Had we got our hands on them, they would have been lucky to face trial.

Robert Mone was a loner and a loser who in the late 1960s was a young soldier with the Gordon Highlanders. He didn't have many friends but what he lacked in companionship he made up in grudge-bearing. He had been expelled from St John's Secondary School in Dundee a few years earlier and bore a strong resentment for the monks who were his teachers there as well as a deep bitterness against the army. He felt that his treatment at their hands had led him to attempt suicide with an overdose of drugs. All it did was make him violently sick. The sickness in his mind was already there.

In November 1967, whilst on leave, Mone went to his old alma mater armed with a shotgun. Filled with hatred and murderous intent, he entered a classroom and despite having had no previous involvement with the young female teacher, Nanette Hanson, held her and her young pupils hostage. An attempt by another teacher to enter the classroom was met with a blast from the shotgun. The siege continued for a few hours until Mone callously shot Nanette Hanson at point-blank range. She died in hospital that afternoon. At his trial, Mone was deemed to be severely schizophrenic and sent to the State Mental Hospital at Carstairs in Lanarkshire. The facility at Carstairs is not a prison. Opened in 1936 for 'mental defectives', it is a detention centre for patients who require, as one mental health act words it, 'treatment under conditions of special security on account of their dangerous, violent or criminal propensities'.

It was here that Mone met Thomas McCulloch. In 1970, McCulloch had shot two workers, a chef and a manageress, at the Erskine Bridge Hotel in Renfrewshire. Fortunately both survived. McCulloch was deemed insane and sent to the State Hospital without limit of time.

For six years, the world heard nothing of Mone and McCulloch. But when it did, it was after a night of horrifying violence during which they murdered three men, wounded three others and terrified a family in a lonely farmhouse. And I would be involved in a grim drive south through a raging blizzard with a gun under my coat and a mission to fulfil.

On 30 November 1976, our Serious Crime Squad team had been sent from our base at Temple Police Office in Glasgow to East Kilbride to assist the local detectives in tracing a youth who had attempted to murder a young woman in a quiet park area. She had been stabbed several times and we were to conduct inquiries in the surrounding area. On arrival at East Kilbride Police Office, the team, comprising Detective Inspector Jock Fleming, Detective Constable Graeme Pearson, Detective Constable Donald Maule and myself, learned of events that night at Carstairs. Mone and McCulloch had escaped using equipment they had made in the hospital workshops over a period of months and stashed away. This equipment included knives, axes, a garrotte, a crossbow and a rope ladder. They also made disguises, including false beards, a nurse's uniform and fake ID. This was clearly a meticulously planned operation by very dangerous, crazy men.

They had pounced on a nursing officer, Neil MacLellan, and a patient, Ian Simpson, throwing paint stripper in their faces. The intention was to get the keys but both men put up a brave fight and were hacked to death. Simpson was known as the A9 Killer, having murdered two men on or near the Highland road in 1962. Deemed insane and unfit to plead, Simpson was sent to Carstairs only to be murdered himself 14 years later. Reports indicate that he redeemed his past sins somewhat by trying to save Mr MacLellan from the bloodlust of their attackers.

Once outside the prison, Mone and McCulloch had feigned a road accident, with one inmate lying on the road and the other, wearing the stolen nurse's uniform, seemingly tending him. They got the result they wanted. A helpful driver stopped. The intention was to steal his car but then a passing police car pulled over. Neither of the officers knew anything about the escape and as they climbed out of their vehicle to see if they could assist, they were attacked by the maniacs. PC John Gillies was wounded but managed to escape with his life, but his neighbour, George Taylor, was hacked at with such force that he was almost decapitated. He staggered along the road and collapsed in front of a local bus. Constable Taylor, aged 27, was the first officer killed on duty since the formation of Strathclyde Police.

As this information filtered through to us in the East Kilbride Office, we were ordered to join the hunt for the triple killers. Duty officers had the ability to issue firearms to qualified officers in appropriate circumstances. However, only two guns were held at East Kilbride and these had already been logged out to local officers for this incident. We returned to Glasgow and were all issued with firearms at the Central Police Office at St Andrew's Street. From there, we received an update from Force Control that the killers had stolen a car and were heading south on the A74. No one was in immediate pursuit at that point. We decided to put that right.

I was driving at speeds well in excess of 90 mph, which, given the severe weather conditions of icy roads and high winds coupled with the seemingly endless roadworks, made it a nightmare of a drive. We were constantly in contact with Force Control. At one point, the Chief Constable, David McNee, came on the air telling us to be very careful when we caught up with the men, as they were known to still be in possession of weapons and they had 'already proved' (which meant that they had already killed) three that night. There was no way that my colleagues and I were going to be additional victims. I, at least, had made up my mind about that. Mone and McCulloch were both armed and dangerous. So were we. If we caught up with them and they gave us the slightest provocation, they were going down.

I've never had to kill a man in the course of duty. On that occasion, I had no doubt that I would do it if I had to. Thankfully, my resolve was not put to the test.

As I steered the car along the icebound A74, Force Control constantly updated us with information. Mone and McCulloch had attacked and stolen a works van but had abandoned it in a muddy field, leaving its driver and passenger injured in the back. They then forced their way into a farmhouse and terrorised the farmer and his family before stealing their car and heading south. Strathclyde Police notified forces further south and the police at Carlisle set up a running roadblock. They spotted the car and put a vehicle in front, another behind it and a police van at its side. As they approached a slip road, they ran the stolen van off the road into a field. Mone and McCulloch were, unfortunately, not seriously injured and were carted off to Carlisle Police Office.

We arrived at Carlisle Police Office minutes afterwards. Before going in, we were instructed to unload our weapons, probably for our own safety as well as that of the prisoners. Soon a number of other Scottish officers arrived, having also made the journey south. A police casualty surgeon examined the prisoners and declared their injuries were consistent with having been involved in a road accident. He deemed them fit for custody and they were handed over to us. Thankfully, I did not have to drive back up the road, although I did have to share the back seat with Robert Mone.

On the drive up to Scotland, he boasted of how they had managed to make the weapons in the workshops at Carstairs, also saying that they had forged passports and that they had a stash of gold krugerrands. He was totally happy with what had happened that night apart from the fact that he was back in custody. It was a difficult journey, as it was hard to keep my hands off him because of his boasting and his clear satisfaction at the carnage he had perpetrated that day.

McCulloch came up in a separate car and, along with Mone, was taken into custody at Lanark Police Office, where they were charged with the three murders and all associated crimes. After being thoroughly examined by a variety of doctors and psychiatrists, they were then deemed sane and fit to plead. They were later convicted of all charges and received life sentences.

This was certainly one of the most trying days I spent as a police officer. My career was built on chasing and catching killers and other crooks. However, this was the one occasion where if I had caught them I would have had no compunction about leaving them dead. Even now, over 30 years after those terrifying events, I can feel the cold rage creep up on me as I think of them.

AN EXERCISE IN TERROR

It was only when I joined the Serious Crime Squad that I first really became aware of the work of the SAS. Of course, I'd heard of the Special Air Service but it wasn't until I played a terrorist in joint training exercises with the fire service, ambulance personnel and intelligence agencies that I realised just how professional and efficient they are.

During one particular two-day exercise, I was holed up in a derelict building with other would-be terrorists and several hostages. One senior officer decided that he would be a hero and walk forward to the front gate of the building. Calling through a loudhailer, he insisted that we should give ourselves up. I radioed the controllers and asked if I was allowed to shoot him. The response was that it was a bloody good idea. I leaned out of the window and fired a blank at him. One of the marshals walked over, tapped him on the shoulder and told him to lie down on the soaking-wet grass in his beautifully pressed uniform, as he was now 'dead'. He lay there for about half an hour until it was negotiated with us that he could be carried away on a stretcher. The Chief Constable, Pat Hamill, was there as an observer and was not best pleased with the idiotic performance of this man.

I was involved in further situations with SAS personnel and came to admire their dedication – although they could take it too far. The exercises were for me a bit of light relief – until the soldiers kicked the living shit out of me during the final stages, leaving me covered in bruises from head to toe. They, unlike policemen, were not taught how to hold back – or, indeed, they were not expected to do so. I think it was difficult for them to switch from real-life situations to training situations. The exercises had a very serious aspect and we were all expected to inject as much realism as possible into these scenarios. That day, for me, there was just a little too much realism, or maybe they just didn't like the polis!

During the second exercise I took part in, I was again a 'terrorist'; the SAS were to storm the house we were in to end the siege. They did this by blowing out the windows then lobbing in stun grenades, known as flash-bangs. This was so realistic that the stairs in the house were set on fire and everyone had to be evacuated via a ladder from the first-floor window. I was taken with the other 'terrorists' by the SAS soldiers into the middle of an adjacent field and debriefed. I learned that they were the same squad who, months earlier (in May 1980), had been involved in the Iranian Embassy Siege.

GUN CRIME

As a detective sergeant in the Serious Crime Squad, in charge of an armed team, one of my specific remits was to respond to gun crime. At the time, the Norval Govan team was running riot throughout the city and they inevitably spawned copycat gun crimes.

The original Serious Crime Squad was made up of detectives known for their ability to gather information from the criminal community, and they were rather good at it. However, the city is a big place and it is not always possible to second-guess the criminal as to his next target. The three groups within the Serious Crime Squad were constantly vying with one another to come up with the best information. Our touts were known to the criminals as 'grasses', one word being benign, the other malignant: it all depends on your viewpoint. Information from touts came in many forms. It might give the time and date of a specific crime or relate more generally to a series of crimes being committed.

Just after 10 a.m. one morning, my squad was cruising the city centre when a call came through on the radio about an armed hold-up taking place at a bookmaker's in Forge Street. Two armed men had entered and threatened the staff with sawn-off shotguns. They had stolen the previous day's takings.

The raiders had run off in the direction of the high flats at the top of Forge Street, closely pursued by three employees from a nearby butcher's shop, who had been alerted by the screams of the female staff from within the bookmaker's. The butchers had identified the block of flats the neds had entered and, very cleverly, two of them had stationed themselves at opposite corners so that they could see the complete perimeter of the building. The other butcher relayed information to the police by phone from the concierge's office.

On our arrival, we found we had been beaten to it. There was already a strong uniformed presence at the flats. John Blincow, the head of the Serious Crime Squad, and the CID boss of the division had decided on the strategy of having each house visited by officers, working from the bottom up. As there were roughly 80 in the block, this attempt to isolate where the neds had gone to ground was going to take some time. It had also been decided that if there was no answer at a door, a uniformed cop would be stationed outside it.

This operation attracted strong media attention. There were soon television camera crews on site as well as print journalists and photographers eager to report on what had grown into a full-scale siege situation.

The Serious Crime Squad was the armed response team for Strathclyde at that time, but we were being backed up by the firearms force training instructors, two of whom had turned up in their full metal jacket kit, looking like something from the SAS training manual. Our guns were always hidden from view, whereas when the instructors turned up theirs were in full view – pump-action shotguns, with side arms strapped to their legs. Dozens of cameras clicked and whirred when they arrived. The press were having a field day.

By the time the search had reached the seventh floor, several apparently empty houses had been identified. On the sixth floor, the door of one of these suddenly opened and two neds came out with their hands in the air. Needless to say, the cop standing there got the fright of his life but they simply handed him a bag containing a shotgun and a large sum of money. We arrived and huckled the neds down into waiting police cars. After short, sharp interviews, these two young criminals told us that there was still a third gang member in the house who had refused to leave; he was still in possession of some of the money. He might also have been armed.

The bosses held a huddled conference on the ground floor. Their decision was conveyed to me by Mr Blincow. Blincow was an excellent old-school cop, and his instructions were brief and to the point. 'Jackson,' he said, 'you and your team go up there and pull that fucker out of that house – now!' Such an approach is very different from modern thinking: nowadays, risk assessment and health and safety would have to be considered before even the most tentative steps were taken, and in my opinion that can sometimes impede good police work.

My team consisted of three other Serious Crime Squad officers and myself. We were taught at firearm training to think of the types of situations we could find ourselves in. A lot of them entailed entering flats such as this. We constructed a scenario where two would go in high, and two low. This was to make sure we did not shoot each other! Before we went upstairs, I was approached by one of the firearms training instructors, who asked if he could back us up as we entered the house. This sounded like a good idea, so the five of us made our way upstairs to the door concerned.

In those days, when you had to enter premises forcefully, it was not with some type of mechanical device that the softies have now but with the solid thump of a well-placed kick under the lock of the door. Hush Puppies weren't much good and it must never be tried with your shoulder – that ends up doing you more damage than anything else!

The door flew open at the first or second kick. If there is someone inside with a gun, it is not clever to knock politely. A young man was framed at the end of the hallway. We all had our guns pointed in his direction and were barking instructions at him to stand still and put his hands in the air. Instead, he stepped out of our line of sight away from the door opening. I reacted first and charged up the hallway into the room, intercepting him as he was reaching towards a coat lying over the back of a couch. I grabbed him and we both went flying over the back of the settee, which up-ended with the force of my attack. I landed on top of him and in order to subdue him gave him a fair pummelling. I had been joined by one of my colleagues, who had his gun pointed squarely between the ned's eyes, as we shouted for him to stop struggling and behave himself.

Then I heard the unmistakable, metallic sound of a shotgun being ejected behind me.

It's a sound distinctive enough to make you wet yourself. My first thought was that the two neds had lied – that there were really two guys in the flat. I whirled round ready to throw myself out of the way only to see the firearms instructor standing at the door to the main room. He had been used to action in a training scenario – the speed of a real-life situation had caught him by surprise. In the excitement, he had mistakenly ejected a cartridge from his shotgun. Thankful that it wasn't a gun-crazy thug, I sent him out of the way to check the rooms with the other detectives. We found some of the money but no gun.

As I later recounted this tale, a friend came away with the couthy comment, 'A case of premature ejaculation!'

six

Seven Years in the Gorbals

I was in the Serious Crime Squad for only two years before being promoted to the rank of detective inspector and posted to the Southern Division, where I took up duty in the Gorbals sub-division. I relished the challenge of having my own area to deal with. The Gorbals, home to many known, hard criminals, was renowned far and wide as a tough area, which suited me down to the ground.

Most of my bosses were happy to let me and my team get on with the job but there was one in particular who would try to catch us out by appearing very early on Sunday mornings when his wife had obviously kicked him out to get the newspapers. He would have done better had he appeared at lunchtime when, after all our work was cleared, we would head for the Stirling Castle pub for some light relief. The Gorbals is a heavy place to work and it was necessary to have a small break.

During the seven years I spent there, the serious inquiries I headed were cleared up and the detection rate for crimes overall rose significantly. This was down to a good hard-working team and good old-fashioned detective work.

It was here that I took charge of my first murder inquiry as a senior investigating officer, or SIO. It was unprecedented for a detective inspector to handle such a case, whereas nowadays, detective inspector is often the highest rank involved in serious inquiries. This particular case concerned the vicious killing of a young boy whose family had recently moved to Castlemilk housing scheme. Three sons of a neighbouring family, for no reason other than the fact he was a newcomer, battered him to death with paving stones. It was a meaningless, thoughtless and callous crime that prompted a riot in the neighbourhood as locals expressed their contempt for the family responsible. Our first job was to find witnesses and secure statements. This and other evidence led us to the three brothers, who were soon locked up.

It is crucial when dealing with neds to listen closely to the way they speak and the phrases they use. In this case, when I was charging the youths with murder, none of them made any reply to the charge. But when I went on to ask if any of them required a lawyer, the oldest brother said, 'I would need Petrocelli to get me out of this.' I duly noted this comment and it was taken in court as an admission of guilt. I had to explain to the trial judge, however, that Petrocelli was an American TV lawyer who was always getting his clients found not guilty on seemingly impossible cases. The brothers really did need such a lawyer, because at the end of the day they all got life sentences.

I also locked up five others for mobbing and rioting – this gang had attacked the family house of the neds I locked up for the murder and so I was able to clear Castlemilk of lots of hooligans in one fell swoop. I was well satisfied with that night's work.

DEATH OF CATWEASEL

One winter's night in 1978, I received a phone call telling me that a man's body had been found in a flat in a high-rise block in the Gorbals. Having separated from his wife, the registered tenant was staying with a friend in the Saracen area of the city. He said he had discovered the corpse when he came back to the unoccupied flat to collect his mail.

Uniform shift officers arrived first and called for the CID. Once the on-duty detectives had seen the extremely bizarre murder scene, they telephoned me at home. When I arrived, I found the dead man lying naked on the bed in a cruciform position. He had been stabbed a number of times in the chest and strangled with a piece of clothesline that was still around his neck. But worse than this, and highly unusually, his penis had been cut off and shoved into his mouth along with a great quantity of his pubic hair.

The first task was to identify the dead man and this turned out to be rather easy, as his clothing was lying on the floor. Documents were found in his pocket that showed he lived on the same floor of the block of flats. We learned that he had stayed there with his mother but he had stolen so much from her that she had thrown him out. He had since become a bit of a tramp. We knew we would have to have the body formally identified and the obvious choice for this was his mother. However, how do you ask a woman to identify the body of her son when it was in such a state? Detective Sergeant Simpson 'Simmy' Henderson and I approached her door with some trepidation, wondering how we could broach the subject of the death of her son and seek a positive identification. It was going to be rather tricky to say the least.

A middle-aged woman wearing a dressing gown answered our knock. Behind her, we could see a gentleman in his vest and pants. The embarrassed couple quickly explained to us that they were old friends and had met in the pub that evening, he having just returned to the Gorbals after a long sea voyage, and they were just catching up on old times. However, the man's presence actually helped us out of the tricky situation, as he knew the son and came with us to identify him. This man's last words to us that evening were that he had not been in the Gorbals for three years and this had been some homecoming. He vowed not to return for at least another three years.

The householder who had found the body had been taken to Gorbals Police Office. I learned from him that he was staying with a newly married mate and his young wife in the north side of the city. Further questioning led to the revelation that he was in love with his mate's wife and that they were, in fact, having a wee fling. However, three nights before this, the husband had wanted to be alone with his wife as it was her birthday, and he had asked his friend to take a hike. Consumed with jealousy, the peeved householder had decided to make his sorry way over to his own abode in the Gorbals, only to find the way into his house blocked by a man sleeping on his doormat. This person turned out to be the local down-and-out known as Catweasel, after the well-known television show. Then, very strangely, he had invited the tramp into his home to sleep for the night on a chair in the living room while he himself went to bed in the bedroom.

He alleged that during the course of the night he had woken up to find the tramp in bed beside him trying to have sex with him. Horrified by this overture, he had set about his molester, stabbing him in the chest, strangling him with a clothes rope, then hacking off his penis with a pair of blunt kitchen scissors and stuffing the offending member into the murdered man's mouth. He said he'd thrown the scissors down a drain. I arranged for the sewers in the vicinity to be searched and the bloody, blunt scissors were recovered in a duct near the flats.

He said he had returned to his home three days after the murder and reckoned that he could fool the police into believing he had just stumbled across the body by accident. However, it's amazing what a session in a police interview room can do to a man's resolve – especially when the man in question is not a hardened criminal.

He was charged with murder and later that year appeared at the High Court in Glasgow. He gave evidence in his own defence, stating that the tramp had tried to have sex with him and that this had provoked his violent reactions. This was clearly a tactic to represent his actions as justifiable homicide or, at the very least, culpable homicide in the hope that he would either walk free or receive a fairly light sentence. He nearly convinced the jury but after careful consideration they found him guilty of the murder and he received a life sentence.

I believe that this man was so sexually frustrated and angry on the particular night that he had gone to bed willingly with the tramp but then became so disgusted with his own actions that he had committed the murder.

A rider to this story was that many years later, after he had been released, my wife Katie and I were invited to a function at a hotel owned by friends of ours, who mentioned that someone who was working in the hotel had been done for murder in the Gorbals. It turned out to be the same guy. I saw him that night, handing round food to the guests. If he recognised me, he didn't let on but, given the knowledge I had of his crime, I had absolutely no appetite for the cocktail sausages he was dispensing.

A GORBALS WEDDING

Midday on a Saturday was usually a busy time in the Gorbals Office because we would be clearing up the myriad incidents from the previous night. On one occasion when there had – unusually – been nothing really serious on the Friday night, four of us decided to treat ourselves to a curry. Our chosen curry house was the Koh-I-Noor, which had the double attraction not only of serving the best Indian food in town at a special lunch rate but also of being on Gibson Street up the West End, not sitting in our area. Most members of the old Glasgow CID were curry aficionados, and my mouth was certainly shaped for something hot and spicy that particular day.

We went downstairs from the CID rooms and passed through the public bar area, so called not because it provided a nice line in ales and spirits but because it was nothing more than a bar at which the public stood to have any queries answered. A rather irate member of the public was speaking to the bar officer.

'When's this ambulance coming tae the Cumberland, big man?' the man asked, referring to the Cumberland Arms pub, which was almost next door.

'Why do you need an ambulance?' he was asked.

'There's a punter bleeding to death on the pub floor and we cannae get served because of the mess.'

We headed for the pub and, sure enough, found a man lying on his side, bleeding profusely from a severe leg wound. Luckily, one of the other customers had some knowledge of first aid and had used his tie as a tourniquet but there was still a fair amount of blood around and things didn't look too good. The only saving grace was that he was on the tiled area of the floor and not on the carpet, so the mess was slightly contained. This being a Gorbals pub, it didn't prevent the punters from getting the bevvy in – they simply stepped over him to place their orders with the barman. Meanwhile, a singsong was being conducted in the snug area. It could only happen in Glasgow.

There was still no sign of an ambulance. I suddenly remembered that there was a standing instruction that no ambulance would attend a public house in the Gorbals unless the police were already present, due to the number of assaults on ambulance personnel. The man on the floor was obviously bleeding to death and swift action was required. I sent one of my team back to the office for a couple of prisoners' blankets and the police van. We quickly moved the injured man onto the blankets then into the back of the van and he was carted off to the Victoria Infirmary.

With the victim off for treatment, we had to sort out what had happened. When the police arrived in a Gorbals pub, the clientele invariably attempted to leave for a variety of reasons, not least being that many had outstanding arrest warrants. A tried and tested means of preventing this type of mass exodus is to immediately close the pub doors – not rocket science but it works. The potential witnesses duly captured, forensics and photographers were sent for and interviews with staff and customers commenced. What we learned might appear to be bizarre but this was the Gorbals. It was discovered that the previous night had not been as quiet as we had thought.

The Cumberland Arms had an upstairs lounge that had been booked the previous evening for a wedding reception, the ceremony having taken place earlier that day. The bride's parents had taken the precaution of hiring a bouncer to ensure that no gatecrashers tried to obtain free booze, a common enough precaution, but they had chosen a 45-year-old hard man just out of Barlinnie after having served five years for attempted murder, who was now trying to re-establish his reputation in the Gorbals hierarchy.

The reception apparently went swimmingly until about 9.30 p.m. That was when a local headcase and real hard man, 'Big Dan', appeared on the scene with a pal. Big Dan was big in every way but his brain capacity. He stood 6 ft 2 in. tall and weighed in at approximately 18 stones, whereas the hired bouncer was 5 ft 7 in. and built like a Biro pen. Nevertheless, the older man took his role very seriously and confronted Dan and his friend, telling them that they were not welcome, as they had not received an invitation. Dan tried to brush past the bouncer and make his way to the bar. At this, the bouncer lifted a Guinness bottle from the bar and attempted to smash it over Dan's head, little realising the bottle was merely for display and made of light plastic. Big Dan proceeded to knock seven colours of shite out of the wee man, blacking both his eyes and breaking his nose. Eventually, the ruckus calmed down and the reception continued.

The following day, the Saturday, it had been arranged that both parties would meet in the public bar of the Cumberland Arms to settle their differences and agree to let sleeping dogs lie. As normally happens in such circumstances, the two adversaries adjourned to the toilet, where they gave each other a cuddle and a few tears were shed over the previous night's events. Both apologised profusely, each stating he was not aware of the other's reputation. On returning to the bar, Big Dan bought the older man a pint to make up for his sore face then continued drinking with his friends at the bar, not giving a monkey's, while the older man sat on his own, nursing his pint and his anger.

When the time was right and Big Dan was in mid-swallow of his third pint, the wee man made his move, darting across the pub floor and plunging a dagger into Dan's exposed belly. He managed two strikes, both causing serious wounds to Dan's abdomen, before the big man reacted. He grabbed the knife and again an uneven struggle ensued, resulting in Dan using the wee man's dagger against him by stabbing him in the leg, severing a main artery. Dan bolted from the pub when he realised how seriously injured he himself was and one of his friends drove him to the Victoria Infirmary. On checking, we learned that he had indeed booked in there and was awaiting an emergency operation on his stomach wounds.

We had managed to contain all of the pub's customers and were obtaining statements from them. This was a normal Gorbals Saturday-afternoon clientele in a busy pub with something in the region of 60 to 100 customers present when the assaults took place. I was, however, astonished to learn that this pub had massive toilet facilities unequalled throughout Scotland – as all of the customers stated they were in there when the stabbings took place.

I made my way to the Victoria Infirmary to find out how my clients, or victims, were holding up and to advise the hospital staff not to house them in the same ward should they survive, as they might start setting about one another with their bedpans. I came across the wee man lying on a trolley in the corridor of the emergency department, trussed up like a chicken in a foil survival blanket, apparently out for the count. I began to speak to the nurse attending to him, telling her what had occurred, all the while gauging the patient's reaction.

'He's comatose due to his injury,' the nurse said.

'That right?' I said and gave the figure on the trolley a glance. I saw his eyelids flickering, which may have been something to do with the coma but I really didn't think so.

'Would you mind if I tried to have a wee word with him?'

She shrugged. 'Go ahead, it'll not do any harm – but you'll get no reaction.'

I leaned over the trolley and whispered in the man's ear, 'Dan's having an operation just now and if he dies I will be charging you with murder.'

The reaction was instantaneous. He sat bolt upright on the trolley, denying the intention of murder. I was not quite as impressed as the nurse by his amazing recovery. Perhaps I missed my calling as a faith healer.

Dan survived the procedure and I spoke to him the following day in hospital. He insisted his actions had been in self-defence but due to the circumstances leading up to the knife fight, I decided to charge each of them with attempting to murder the other and let the courts sort it out. However, following the law of the street, they would not speak up in court against each other, so the cases were dismissed.

But it was annoying that I had missed out on a lovely bhuna lamb lunch.

THE HAMPDEN RIOT

When you are a police officer in Glasgow, it is very difficult to avoid policing football matches at some level. Whilst working as a uniformed officer, along with the rest of my shift, I was sometimes detailed to attend big matches at Hampden, Ibrox or Celtic Park. Only the main stand was seated in those days and because the club officials did not stick to the designated maximum capacity, spectators were crushed in like sardines. There were no large teams of stewards as there are today and it was the remit of the police to keep order at these events. We were supposed to keep the passageways clear – an impossible task. If you were a young, inexperienced cop, as I was then, you were sent down near the front by older colleagues. It didn't take long to realise why, as you were soon up to your ankles in the urine that flowed freely down the terraces. On one occasion, I was asked to assist in jailing a miscreant who had inadvertently peed down an older colleague's leg. Toilets, if you could call them that, were seldom used because punters didn't want to lose their spots on the terraces.

Another good tip while policing these games was always to wear your raincoat at a match. The reason for this was that if you had to arrest someone from the crowd it was invariably from around where their friends were standing, so you would find after locking up the ned that your back would be covered in spit. It's not a charming fact but it's a fact nevertheless.

Later in my career, my seven-year tenure as detective inspector at the Gorbals took in many matches. It was my responsibility to delegate detective officers to various sections of the ground during large matches at Hampden and to update my divisional commander and detective superintendent regarding crimes reported during the game. One match that stands out for all the wrong reasons was the 1980 Scottish Cup final between Celtic and Rangers.

Football in Scotland in this period was dominated by Aberdeen under the management of Sir Alex Ferguson. This Cup final was therefore a match that meant everything to the Old Firm clubs. It was the only chance of either team lifting silverware that season. With their bitter rivalry and their fanatical supporters, it should have been obvious that trouble could be brewing. Long before the game started, Hampden was full of supporters well fired up on various alcoholic beverages – people were still allowed to carry booze into football matches. The hatred began spilling over before the kick-off and as the alcohol level rose, so did the body count of fans being locked up. The sectarian singing was at full blast as the two teams took to the field. If you wanted a quiet Saturday afternoon, this was definitely not the place to be.

I generally stood near to the players' tunnel and was accompanied, on this occasion, by a plain-clothes policeman, Tom Paterson, who was attached to the CID as an aide. During the game, Tom and I would gather statistics for the match commander concerning crimes such as serious assaults, pocket-picking – which was a regular occurrence – and other incidents in which the CID usually became involved. This information was relayed directly to me by radio to be passed on up the line and was only part of a host of other information the match commander had to deal with. The match commander on this day was my own divisional commander, Chief Superintendent Hamish McBean, a true policeman who appreciated working cops and who was in turn appreciated by them.

Also present were the Chief Constable, Sir Patrick Hamill, and his deputy, Willie McMaster. This was a trifle unusual to say the least but it served to keep all police officers on their toes. Little did lowly placed officers such as myself realise that a new system was about to be tried regarding the policing of matches. Needless to say, this particular day was not the best time to move away from tried and tested methods.

In the past, a match such this, with something in the region of 70,000–80,000 supporters within the ground, would be attended by around 500 police officers. Strathclyde Police had always been proud of its reputation for crowd control and was certainly admired for it by other forces. The match itself was not a thrilling spectacle, as the players seemed to be more interested in not losing than in winning. It was the usual Old Firm encounter full of hard tackles and snarling players, which of course got the crowd more raucous and excitable, but with no goals. From a police viewpoint, a no-scoring draw is generally a good result in that it tends to take some of the sting out of the crowd's behaviour and things settle down quite reasonably. Even though this was a Celtic–Rangers encounter it seemed to be heading that way. Boy, were we wrong.

The game was drawing to a close with only a couple of minutes of extra time to be played when George McCluskey of Celtic latched onto a through ball and scored the only goal of the game. It was a case of light the green touchpaper and stand well back. The goal had been scored at the Celtic supporters' end of the ground and McCluskey continued his run onto the track and towards the Celtic support, waving as he went. Some Celtic fans decided to take this as an invitation to join him on the pitch, which they duly did, causing all hell to break loose.

I was still standing at the tunnel at this point. Due to the fact that the game was about to end, many of the television camera crews and news photographers had gathered there for interviews and photos of the players as they left the pitch, as would have been normal. This, however, was no longer a normal situation. The Rangers support obviously saw the Celtic fans invading the pitch. The words 'red flag' and 'bull' sprang to mind. They charged from their end and within seconds the pitch became a seething mass of brawling fans. My first reaction was to look after the officials and players – not to mention the only girl in the immediate vicinity, part of a TV crew. My thoughts were to get them safely into the tunnel and out of the firing line.

Apparently, it had been decided during headquarters match-planning that rather than keep all officers inside the ground until the finish of the game, as was normal practice, half the strength would be removed during the middle of the second half and dispatched to their delegated duties outside. It was a clever way to save money but not to stop trouble. And trouble there certainly was, as the crowd continued to batter lumps out of one another as well as the police officers, who were struggling to control the escalating incident. The officers were doing their level best but they could not contain the violence.

There was one senior officer present, Detective Superintendent Ian Smith, who realised that drastic situations required drastic solutions. He called for the return of the Mounted Branch personnel, who were on their way back to the stables as part of the money-saving exercise. Contact was made as the dozen or so mounted officers were travelling along Cathcart Road. They wheeled round and galloped post-haste back to Hampden.

Their return to the arena was a sight to behold. They were led by a chief inspector who obviously relished the scene, imagining this as the Charge of the Light Brigade, and ordered the officers to draw their long batons and charge the hooligans on the pitch. The effect was amazing. The mob took to their heels and made for the relative safety of the terraces, away from these massive steeds. From there, though, they continued to lob all sort of objects at the police and press photographers. The Mounted Branch had come in like the cavalry but unfortunately in the melee a police horse, ridden by a female officer later referred to as 'the heroine of Hampden', trampled an officer on the ground, breaking his leg.

One of the favoured alcoholic drinks of the neds of this era was Pomagne: fizzy, apple-flavoured and cheap, it came in litre bottles with an extremely thick and heavy base, making them very dangerous weapons. These bottles, generally empty due to their consumption during the match, were hurled at the police on the trackside. At the Rangers end of the ground, a *Daily Record* photographer named Eric Craig, who was recording the events, was struck on the head by one of these flying bottles. Probably because he was so intent on taking photographs, he didn't see it coming. He sustained a severe depressed fracture to his skull and was very lucky that he did not die from the blow.

Meanwhile, I was still at the tunnel entrance surveying the carnage with Constable Tom Paterson. In my detective clothing of a blue lounge suit, I felt that had I walked onto the pitch, I was likely to be crowned by a police baton. However, my attention was drawn to a particular ned dressed in grey trousers and top who was running about taking flying kicks at cops who were on the ground wrestling with hooligans. Tom and I saw him at the same time and we both had the same thought: 'He's getting the jail.' Taking our lives in our hands, we marched onto the pitch and seized hold of the ned; he threw a punch but got flattened for his efforts. We were most surprised when, as we roughly hauled him away, the crowd in the main stand stood to a man and cheered like hell. They had obviously not been amused by his antics either. I had thought that because of the mayhem around us, no one had witnessed the left uppercut that had caused his malaise.

The following week, I was given the task of trying to identify the culprit who had thrown the bottle that had caused the damage to Eric Craig. It was, in actual fact, an attempted murder during a major incident that had received national coverage. The only way that I could perhaps identify the proverbial needle in a haystack was to approach the various news agencies and request that they supply me with all footage and photographs. The media responded quite readily and soon my small office in the Gorbals was festooned with photos of the riot in its various stages.

I also obtained video footage from the BBC. This was extremely helpful, as at one point the camera was focused on the mounted policewoman and her male colleague as they galloped around the track near the Rangers end where Eric Craig was standing, and I managed to get a clear view of him seconds before he was struck. Unfortunately, I could not spot the bottle hurler and he was never caught. After a long period of convalescence, Eric Craig was able to return to his post at the *Daily Record*.

The series of photographs told many stories of what had occurred that afternoon. One was of an older policewoman delivering a motherly smack to the side of a young ned's head, and the look on his face showed his lack of appreciation at the pain inflicted by the stiff right-hander. I recognised an old colleague of mine from the Northern Division, John Staunton, a no-nonsense type of cop who had had more commendations from the Chief Constable than I have had hot dinners. He was a great neighbour to have at your side in a tricky situation. John was on his own, standing behind the goal at the Celtic end, facing the howling mob of fans as they invaded the pitch and ran riot. He had managed to get hold of a corner flag and was setting about the neds with great gusto, enthusiastically trying to stem the tide of hooligans on his own. I was reminded of Samson setting about his assailants with the jawbone of the ass in the film *Samson and Delilah*; many of John's assailants, each and every one of them an ass, were lying on the grass around him, nursing their own jawbones. John Staunton was, I believe, a staunch Celtic supporter but this did not prevent him from going by the old police adage: 'A ned is a ned whatever colour he may be wearing, or whatever his background.'

The 1980 Cup final debacle directly led to a change in legislation whereby alcohol was banned from football matches and a number of strictures were put in place to limit the effect that alcohol and the associated disorder would have on future similar events in Scotland. Undoubtedly, this has been hugely successful. I spoke to Chief Superintendent McBean in the immediate aftermath of the game and he was not in favour of the headquarters edict with regard to the deployment of officers. The Chief Constable and Deputy Chief were both, to use a football term, as sick as parrots after what had occurred. They were obliged to rethink the new strategy, which had obviously been presented to them by some academic or office-bound police officers.

A LAXATIVE ATTITUDE

Tom Paterson, the young cop with whom I'd arrested the ned on the pitch at Hampden, was one of my best officers and a natural thief-catcher. Tom suffered from a stomach ulcer and always had a biscuit or a piece of chocolate in his pocket to, as he put it, feed his ulcer. In my department, he was sometimes neighboured with Detective Sergeant Simpson Henderson. Simmy was from the Highlands and had hair the colour of a Highland coo; he wore it in what used to be called 'a coo's lick' – a big wave at the front. Simmy was also a bit of a hog and always took great delight in stealing Tom's biscuit or chocolate. This, needless to say, pissed Tom off a lot.

Tom had gone back to uniform for a brief spell and during this period his mind had been working overtime thinking how he could get back at Simmy. He bought a bar of Ex-Lax from a chemist and wrapped it in some Cadbury's wrapping-paper, hoping to entice Simmy to have a small piece. Tom was standing at the back door of Gorbals Police Office with another officer as Simmy was coming on duty, and just happened to produce his chocolate. True to form, Simmy made a grab for it and he didn't just eat a piece, he scoffed the whole bar in one go.

Simmy was due to report several cases to the Procurator Fiscal that morning and when he came into the office, he snaffled the keys for one of the cars. Shortly afterwards, with the productions officer, he headed for the Sheriff Court to lodge his paperwork and productions (items seized in the course of an inquiry). This can take up to an hour or so. On the way back from the court buildings, his driving became very erratic and he drove straight through the lights at Gorbals Cross, causing havoc to other road users in his dash to reach the haven of the office toilets. He scared the living daylights out of the productions officer, who was white with fright and had no need for laxatives.

Simmy remained in the toilet for the best part of half an hour. Tom told me about the chocolate and I went in and spoke to him through the door and asked him for the keys for the car. He slid them out under the door and then appeared, ashen-faced, with his generally immaculate red hair over his eyes. Not letting on that I knew what had happened, I asked if he was feeling OK. He came away with the wonderful line that the previous night he had had a couple of vodkas and lemonade, and the lemonade must have been off.

When Simmy eventually learned what had really happened, a war of attrition in various forms took place before peace was restored with Gorbals Office.

THE CASE OF THE MISSING FOOT

The Govanhill area threw up some very interesting, strange and sometimes bizarre inquiries. Curiously, I can't recall ever being called to an inquiry in that area when it wasn't dark and raining.

One evening, the beatman (the officer patrolling the area) was called to a flat in an old-style tenement block, where the occupant had noticed a small, dark stain appearing on his ceiling; he reckoned it might be blood. The beatman noticed a trail of blood on the stairs leading past the caller's house. He followed it and found it stopped at a door on the landing above. He knocked but there was no answer. He then decided it was a matter for CID.

When I arrived, I saw that there was not just a blood trail but also bloodstained palm and fingerprints smeared on the walls and steps. Still there was no answer to the door but a large size nine judiciously applied under the lock soon fixed that problem. The flat was what was commonly called a single-end – a hallway leading from the front door to a bedroom and kitchen. The kitchen was where we found the dead man.

He was fully clothed, propped up against a table leg in an almost drunken pose. The only obvious wound was to his left foot; the shoe was missing and a considerable amount of blood was seeping through his sock. We left the corpse undisturbed and began to poke around the rest of the sparsely furnished flat. This is when we got a real shock. On going through to the bedroom, we found sitting in the middle of the floor a severed human foot and, beside it, a set of metal steps and two sets of bloody nail scissors.

Naturally, we had a number of processes and procedures to go through. We contacted the forensic and photographic departments, the casualty surgeon and the on-call Procurator Fiscal, who turned out to be a rather squeamish lady. When she examined the locus, she was visibly horrified at the sight of the bloody foot and took her leave hurriedly, saying that we could leave a report for her in the morning. Once the house had been thoroughly photographed and forensically examined, the detectives started to get down to examining all of the available evidence. We removed the bloody sock from the dead man's left leg and this revealed that his foot was missing. The foot in the bedroom was a left foot, so, being very clever, we assumed that it was the missing one, a deduction of which Sherlock Holmes would have been proud.

That was the easy part. Now we had to find out what the hell had happened to give us this undeniably very strange case. Both the steps and the scissors in the bedroom were found to have slivers of skin and tissue attached to them. Had someone used them to cut off the man's foot? That seemed unlikely. Or had he cut off his own foot? If so, why?

The dead man lived alone and kept himself to himself, but was occasionally seen staggering into the close rather the worse for drink. About three nights before, he had been out on the town drinking with his workmates in their favourite bar in the city centre near Paddy's Market on the Clydeside. He had left them at about 9.30 p.m., saying that he was making his way home, which he generally did on foot. Some of his pals occasionally accompanied him home to continue drinking and they told us that he was prone to taking a short cut across a railway line. This route was examined and a trail of blood spots was found, leading to the dead man's close. Everything was now falling into place. Our man had probably injured himself on the railway line – we assumed an engine had run over his leg. Ultimately, though, this could never be properly established despite the efforts of the railway police to trace any employee who could throw light on the matter, as there was a lot of shunting activity taking place in the area where he probably crossed the lines. However, through the haze of alcohol he had managed to stagger or drag himself home.

All the signs were that he had hauled himself up the stairs on his backside in order to reach his house on the second floor, leaving the bloody fingerprints on the wall and the marks on the steps. Once inside, still steaming drunk but now really beginning to feel the extreme pain pulsing from his wounded ankle, he took some decisive, if grisly action. The foot must have been hanging by the figurative thread and he had probably come to the drunken conclusion that he was liable to feel less pain if he divested himself of the offending appendage. It looked increasingly likely that he had snipped through the remaining pieces of skin and flesh with the small nail scissors before pulling on his sock again, hoping that this would stem the flow of blood. He had then crawled from the bedroom back into the kitchen, where he succumbed to his injury and ultimately died through blood loss. The pain suffered by this man must have been immense but he had died quietly.

You often hear good things spoken of the community spirit in the old tenement closes but it was definitely lacking here. Certainly, the man kept himself to himself but no one bothered about the considerable amounts of blood on the stair. It is too easy for people not to want to become involved with the police. It wasn't until the downstairs neighbour grew annoyed at the stain appearing on his ceiling that any action was taken and by then it was too late.

GORBALS INQUIRY (CIRCA 1902)

Around midnight on a Friday, I was phoned at home and told that we had another murder, this time in the Oatlands district. These calls never bothered me, as I always looked forward to the challenge of helping to solve major crimes. I suppose you could call me a glutton for punishment, but there you go!

The crime scene was a common close in a red sandstone building. I had been beaten to it. Two other officers were standing over the body of a man of around thirty years of age lying face upwards about three yards inside the close, his chest heavily bloodstained. He had been stabbed several times about the body. The entrance to the close was awash with blood.

He had already been identified as a resident who stayed on his own on the first floor. Naturally, that was only the beginning – there was a lot of work to be done. Sometimes, at such loci, some officers will stand looking at the body hoping that by some miracle it will get up and walk away, saving them the trouble of trying to solve the crime.

I stepped out of the close into the street, which was full of police cars and officers. At a close mouth two along from the murder scene, there was a man I recognised as a local worthy, doing his nosey. He signalled to me and I went over to speak to him.

He seemed a bit concerned and asked, 'Am I going to get the jail?'

I asked, 'What for?'

'I'd tried to give some information to a grey-haired detective but he didn't seem interested. He told me to bugger off or I'd get the jail.'

I started to speak to him. First, he asked me the name of the dead person; of course, you must be very cautious in such a situation, so some verbal fencing took place. He actually told me that he thought that he knew who the murdered man was. He was correct in his assumption. He was a veritable mine of information – telling me that the dead man, who originally came from the Gorbals area, had recently split from his wife; she now had a fancy-man. There was bad blood between him and his wife and her boyfriend, whom he named. A good starter for ten! So much for the detective who wouldn't give him the time of day.

We learned from the local cops that the boyfriend stayed with his mother in the Queen Elizabeth Square flats (now demolished), so off we went to pay her a visit. A sweet little old lady answered the door and we enquired as circumspectly as possible as to her boy's whereabouts. She said that she had not seen him for several days. I asked if I could come in and have a wee word with her while my officers had a look around the flat. She reluctantly agreed. As the flat was getting the once-over, we came to a locked bedroom. She told us that it contained nothing but rubbish and that she was unable to open the door. Under the circumstances, the door was forced. The room was not filled with rubbish – it was a little love nest for her son and the wife of the murdered man.

During interviews with the wife and her boyfriend, some startling facts emerged about the sub-culture of the Gorbals, which at that time had an almost village mentality. The Cumberland Arms, although not your typical village pub, was certainly the social hub. Most commonly, if people have a fallout, they stay away from places where they might bump into each other. This did not occur in the Gorbals – the locals were made of sterner stuff and the Cumberland Arms was a melting pot for all kinds of trouble. This was where the wife of the murdered man and her boyfriend had been that Friday evening, ignoring the fact that her estranged husband also drank there.

Apparently, the husband had been a quiet man until he sustained a serious head injury while working on a building site. He became subject to violent mood swings, which she cited as her reason for leaving him. You would expect that she would steer well clear of her estranged husband's watering hole, but not at all. They told us that they had seen her husband at the Cumberland Arms but had not spoken to or had any dealings with him. They stated that they had witnessed a fight in the bar between her husband and another man, the well known local worthy Tam 'the Bam' Lyons. Both had been summarily ejected from the premises and the fight continued on the pavement. The couple were able to name other drinkers who could verify their story. From suspects, the pair had now become potentially vital witnesses.

During the early hours of the morning, the bar manager was contacted and he confirmed their story. This did not immediately let them off the hook, as the locus of the murder was about a mile from the pub, but we did learn that Tam the Bam was also staying in Oatlands at this time. We needed to get a hold of him, so my team and I headed for his abode, a top flat a couple of streets away from the crime scene. We noticed fresh blood on the close walls leading to Lyons' house and more bloodstains on his door.

Police officers are not known for knocking softly but several loud thumps brought no reply. Some of the other officers took the view that we would need to get a warrant to enter. This procedure would have taken time that I felt we did not have. Here's a little-known fact about police work: it is amazing, when faced with such a problem, how some officers with keen senses can detect the smell of gas issuing from a house. I most certainly smelled something that night. To ensure the safety of the other tenants from the leaking gas, I had no qualms about applying my trusty size nine to the door. As it turned out, the flat had an electric cooker but you can't win them all. There was no one inside but we found a bloodstained jacket and shirt. Things were looking bleak for Tam the Bam and good for us.

We arrived back at the locus to find the murder caravan in place outside the crime scene. We had limited manpower at this time of the morning, so we had to prioritise and identify what needed to be done first. I was in favour of the troops going hunting for Tam Lyons.

The early-shift uniformed officers were just coming on duty. All of them knew our Tam. He was the kind of person who would never leave the Gorbals; in fact, he and his friends thought they needed a passport to go to Glasgow Cross. After briefing them about the night's events and the need to capture our prime suspect, I decided to make myself really useful and headed for the shopping arcade at the Queen Elizabeth Square flats to buy some square sausage and some fresh bread rolls for breakfast. As I turned the corner into the shopping arcade, I saw Peter McLeod, an excellent young uniformed cop, and his colleague entering from the other end. Between us stood Tam the Bam and his cronies, drinking from a half-bottle of Four Crown wine. I gave Peter the nod and he and his neighbour quickly captured Tam and took him round the corner to the police office. I continued on my shopping trip and bought my sausages and rolls. Legislation had just been brought out allowing police to hold a suspect for a period of six hours before being charged. Tam the Bam Lyons had the proud honour to be our first beneficiary of this legislation and I didn't have to hurry buying or eating my breakfast!

Tam had taken his last swig of Four Crown for a long time. He told us that after being thrown out of the Cumberland Arms the previous evening, and collecting a second prize in the ensuing fist fight on the pavement, he had acquired a knife and followed his opponent home. There he attacked him in the darkness of his close, stabbing him several times about the body. The knife had then found its way into the nearby River Clyde. He had returned home to change from his bloody clothes before going to a friend's house to finish his drinking session and construct a useless alibi.

He later pled guilty at the High Court in Glasgow.

The author as a police officer in 1960, having
just joined the City of Glasgow Police.

The author (left) and 'Big' John MacDonald leaving
the High Court in Glasgow after the trial of 'Bobo'
Murney and 'Mau-Mau' Morrison in 1968.

I wasn't hunting
Goldie SAYS THOMPSON

By HUGH HINSHELWOOD

WHEN gambling club boss Arthur Thompson (35), who is accused of killing two men, was asked at the High Court in Glasgow if he deliberately forced their van off the road, he replied . . . "A person who does that should be locked up for life for killing two friends."

And smartly dressed Thompson, of Provanmill Road, Glasgow, who said that he had tried three times in his Mark 10 Jaguar to overtake a van which kept blocking him, vigorously denied he was out hunting for James Goldie, one of the dead.

Turning to the Judge, Lord Migdale, he said: "There have been a lot of lies about this but there was no doubt in my mind it was us that was forcing them."

POLICE TELL COURT TWO MEN DIED AFTER JAGUAR DRIVER WAS SEEN 'WAITING HIS CHANCE'

JAMES GOLDIE and PATRICK WELSH: They died in van crash

P.C. JOHN JACKSON: 'Going is very fast'

D.C. JOSEPH JACKSON: 'In car with brother'

'MR. FAIRBAIRN'

Waiting

Arthur Thompson

Not drunk

Heard crash

My friends

Laughing

No joke

Distressed

Scottish Daily Express,
9 November 1966.
The headlines regarding
Arthur Thompson's trial.
(courtesy of the *Scottish Daily Express*)

Arthur Thompson snr at home.
(courtesy of the *Daily Record*)

Arthur Thompson jnr.
(courtesy of the *Daily Record*)

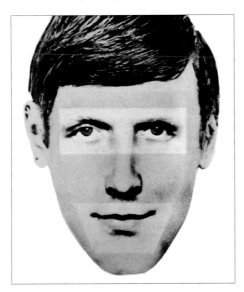

Photofit of 'Bible John'.
(courtesy of the *Daily Record*)

The 'missing foot' case.

An artist's impression of the 'Ibrox Rapist'

Dominic Devine:
the Ibrox Rapist.

The author holding a press conference at Govan Police Office during the Ibrox Rapist inquiry.

Danny 'Scarface' Graham
– the hostage taker.
(courtesy of the *Daily Record*)

Police marksmen at the scene of the hostage situation in Broomloan Court, Govan. (courtesy of the *Daily Record*)

Arthur Thompson jnr.
(courtesy of the *Daily Record*)

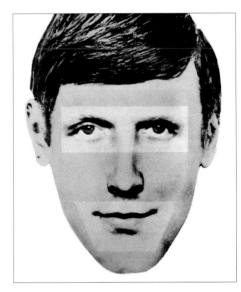

Photofit of 'Bible John'.
(courtesy of the *Daily Record*)

The 'missing foot' case.

Carstairs killer Robert Mone as a young boy.
(courtesy of the *Daily Record*)

Carstairs
killer Thomas
McCulloch.
(courtesy of the
Daily Record)

The cache of weapons made and used by Robert Mone and
Thomas McCulloch at Carstairs, 1976. (courtesy of the *Daily Record*)

Hampden riot, May 1980.
(courtesy of the *Daily Record*)

A victim of the bloody Hampden riot.
(courtesy of the *Daily Record*)

An artist's impression of the 'Ibrox Rapist'.

The author holding a press conference at Govan Police Office during the Ibrox Rapist inquiry.

Dominic Devine: the Ibrox Rapist.

Danny 'Scarface' Graham – the hostage taker. (courtesy of the *Daily Record*)

Police marksmen at the scene of the hostage situation in Broomloan Court, Govan. (courtesy of the *Daily Record*)

Thomas Currie with Ricardo Blanco in the background.
Photograph taken while they were hiring the van.

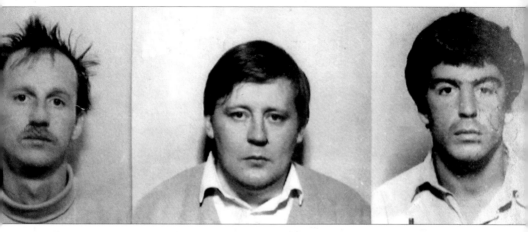

The Kilmarnock Moors Murderers:
Thomas Collins, John Paul McFadyen and Ricardo 'the Hit-man' Blanco.

Ground search about to start at the Burrell Collection building, Pollok Park (Diane McInally murder). (courtesy of the *Daily Record*)

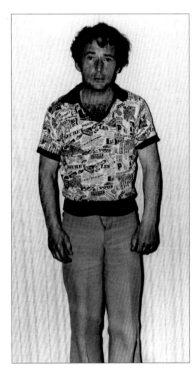

Diane McInally.
(courtesy of the *Daily Record*)

Angus Robertson
Sinclair.

Sex Crimes

The small windowless room is sparsely furnished. There is a table with a scratched surface and four chairs offering little or no comfort, for this is not meant to be a home from home. Nowadays, there is a double-headed tape recorder sitting on the table and sometimes even a video camera high in the corner. These are relatively new additions. In the earlier part of my career, there was me, another officer, the suspect and possibly a solicitor.

It is here in this bare little room that the facts of a case are probed in a bid to draw a confession. Events are examined, sifted and raked over. A good detective knows the right questions to ask and listens for the answers he needs. Queries are repeated to see if answers change. As you listen, it is equally important to watch for responses. Gamblers say that people have 'tells', subtle quirks of expression, twitches or unconscious movements that signal a player is bluffing. Seasoned investigators are always on the lookout for tips that indicate their suspect is lying.

Sometimes, suspects 'burst' and confess all. Sometimes, they hold out for a deal, offering to 'fue in' accomplices in return for leniency. Sometimes, they are as adept as their interrogator, parry the interview technique and coast free. Sometimes, they are so stupid that it's impossible to break through the idiocy barrier. Sometimes, the person is actually innocent.

The easiest suspects to interview are the ones who think that they are really smart and that you are just a dumb cop. One, Ricardo Blanco, springs to mind; he initially made a full confession to the Kilmarnock Moors murder but then thought that by speaking to me again he could somehow get me on his side. In fact, he only talked himself deeper into the shit.

The hardest suspects to interview are undoubtedly women and terrorists. Women can be very thrawn and hard to burst, while terrorists are taught how to deal with interrogation. A combination of the two means you are really up against it. The Brighton bombers, hard-bitten Irish terrorists who attacked the Grand Hotel during the 1984 Conservative Party Conference, were apprehended in a house on the south side of Glasgow. After a week of Special Branch interrogation, all the men were talking but the two women wouldn't even give their names. They were only identified by their fingerprints, which had been found in a terrorist hidey-hole in Northern Ireland. The seasoned interviewers coming out of these interview rooms were dumbfounded by their lack of progress and the women's ability to say nothing.

I know interview rooms well. I've lost count of the number of man-hours I've spent across the table, trying to coax suspects to come clean. I've seen them enter the interview room with confidence and watched them crumble – thieves, rapists, perverts, thugs, killers and terrorists. Empathy is the name of the game. I learned the knack of being able to sense the mood of the suspect. If they got tough, I got tougher. If they were quiet and respectful, so was I. I never lost the head. I never raised a hand. One of my earliest lessons as a cop was that if you ever raise a hand in an interview, you've lost.

With sex offenders, that was a difficult rule to live by.

UNSPEAKABLE CRIMES

In the course of my CID career, I came across certain crimes that were stomach-churning in their wickedness and depravity.

One late shift in the late 1960s, when I was working out of the Northern Division headquarters in Stewart Street, an officer came through from the public bar with two young women in tow, who had said they wanted to talk to a CID officer. They were sisters. The older of the two did most of the talking. Her younger sister, who had a five-year-old son, had recently separated from her husband and was now living with a new man friend. She had confided that she thought he was interfering with her child – although she had left the boy in the house alone with him that night. I was on my feet putting on my jacket when she added, 'Tell the polis what else he does.' The younger sister then poured out an almost unbelievable tale of this guy's other sexual activities. She said he was in the habit of taking stray dogs into a spare bedroom and there had been the unmistakable sound of some type of sexual activity taking place.

She then started kicking up a fuss, saying that he was really a nice man and she loved him; she was sorry she had let her sister talk her into coming to the police and she wanted to go with us to the house. We left them standing on the steps of the police office as we drove off.

The stench of dogs' urine in the filthy close was overpowering. When the man answered the door, we told him that we were police officers and immediately asked where the young boy was. Happily, he was tucked up in bed asleep and OK. We looked through the house and found a bedroom devoid of any furniture apart from a long mirror propped against the wall. We began to question the man regarding his activities with the little boy and when he told us he had 'had the kid play with him a few times', we decided to conduct the rest of the interview at our office. At that point, the sisters arrived in a taxi and we left them in charge of the youngster.

During the interview, the man was very frank about his sexual obsessions. It was bad enough hearing about his interest in the boy but things took a bizarre twist when he proceeded to give an account of his attraction to the canine species. He said it had first occurred when he was in his late teens: travelling on the top deck of a bus going through Bridgeton Cross, he had been aroused at the sight of two dogs copulating. He had subsequently committed countless acts of bestiality. His preference was to allow the dogs to mount him, hence the floor-level mirror – he liked to observe the performance. After he had completed his voluntary statement, he was locked up pending his appearance at court on charges of bestiality and child molestation. The duty officer was in two minds as to whether to lock him up in a cell or the kennels for the night.

He pled guilty to the charges libelled against him and received a requisite jail sentence.

THE BEAST OF THE NORTH

At the time of my initial stint in Northern Division CID, areas such as Sauchiehall Street, West Princes Street, Garnethill, Great Western Road and St George's Road had been plagued by a series of horrible attacks on young girls as they played outside their tenement homes. There had been thirteen sexual assaults on victims ranging in age from eighteen months to five years. The ned responsible took them into basements or occasionally hid them in dustbins until he could find a suitable spot for his perversions. He raped these poor youngsters, using a knife on some of them to make penetration easier. It was a series of vile crimes committed by a vile individual. The media dubbed him 'The Beast of the North'. He was not caught at the time of the rapes and it looked as though he had escaped justice. My boss at this time was a very decent man, Detective Chief Inspector Stuart Fraser. He was an extremely hardy character but as more and more victims were attacked he was deeply affected and eventually left the police early. I have no doubt that these events played heavily on his mind. Over the years, I have known many seasoned police officers to weep at the sights with which they are confronted.

One night, I was working out of Springburn Police Office when the bar officer told me that a man I had dealt with in connection with a previous incident in Blackhill wished to speak to me. He was a decent, hard-working guy who, like any other right-minded individual, had a natural abhorrence for crimes against children.

He had moved in with a woman who had two young daughters. She had apparently suspected her previous partner, James Ferguson, had been interfering with her kids. She had also mentioned that he had seemed very interested in a series of rapes of children on the north side of the city which had stopped around two years before. Ferguson had now returned to the Royston area to live with his mother. He worked on a building site in Bishopbriggs.

I reported all this by phone to DCI Jimmy Bird, who told me to be at his office first thing the next morning. In the meantime, I took steps to have the woman's daughters medically examined and also checked out Ferguson's background. What I discovered seemed to fit. Two weeks before the first attack had taken place, he had been released from Lennox Castle mental institution, where he had been placed for sexual aberrations. When the hospital was contacted during the initial inquiry, the doctors had offered no information regarding Ferguson. When questioned later as to why they had failed to alert us, they stated they thought it would harm their patient's healing process!

The next morning, I arrived at Mr Bird's office on time, if a bit bleary-eyed. I told him what I'd learned about the suspect and also that I had been able to identify the building site on which he worked. Accompanied by Detective Sergeant Tom McShane, DCI Bird and I drove up to the Bishopbriggs building site in the hope of finding Ferguson at work, arriving at around 9 a.m. A foreman pointed Ferguson out to us and we duly detained him. He came along quietly, as the old saying goes. I went to the workman's bothy to collect his jacket and found in an inside breast pocket a small wooden-handled knife. This knife was later forensically examined and found to contain minuscule traces of blood within the wooden handle. Unfortunately, none of these traces could be linked to any of the known victims.

We took Ferguson to the Maitland Street Police Office where he was charged with possession of the knife and held in custody. He was then taken to the boss's room, where we began to question him regarding the attacks upon the children. He had obviously been waiting for this since his arrest and began to open up to us, admitting he was responsible. He even agreed to visit the areas where the attacks had taken place.

Tom McShane and I then took him on a tour of the West End of the city and Ferguson identified streets such as Princes Street, Great Western Road, Woodlands Road and Maryhill Road near to St George's Cross as being places where some of the attacks had occurred. He even took us to a basement in West Princes Street where he had placed a little girl of about four in a dustbin before knifing and raping her. I drove the car while Tom noted everything that Ferguson said. It was a draining experience for both of us. Ferguson recounted, and in some way re-lived – no doubt enjoying all over again – the things he had put children through. It took all our self-control to hold back from inflicting physical harm on him, sick or not.

An identification parade was held that afternoon in Maitland Street. Joe Beltrami, Ferguson's defence lawyer, was present. Several adult witnesses who had been near to the various crime locations and who had seen him run off were able to identify him. When the children who were capable of attending viewed the line-up of men, Ferguson actually identified them from the various places where the rapes had occurred, right in front of his lawyer, who appeared pretty gobsmacked. Identification parades were held in open rooms; there were not yet purpose-built facilities with screens. Ferguson could see the children viewing the parade and when he saw the little girls he was physically aroused and had a visible erection. The medical staff who withheld information should have seen what a creature they had been protecting. Their loyalties had been totally misdirected. Their files on him were horrific and if they had been more forthcoming, perhaps some of these children could have been saved physical injury and lasting trauma. They were unlikely ever to recover from what they had endured at this beast's hands.

Found to be criminally insane and unfit to plead, Ferguson was sent to Carstairs, apparently without limit of time – I say 'apparently', because, as this case shows, you never know what monsters might be deemed sane and healthy and then let loose to prey on society once more.

THE MAN WITH GREEN HAIR

The little girl said that the man had 'spotty green hair and green ears'. He had tried to lure her into a close but she had taken fright and run away. This ten year old was the only lucky one. Other little girls not so fortunate had been brutally assaulted and raped by this man. His victims had all been so young and so traumatised that they had only managed sketchy descriptions of their assailant but this plucky little girl told us he had spotty green hair and green ears. And dirty shoes – but not the usual kind of dirt, she said. She said he was small and – green spots apart – dark-haired. She told us what he was wearing. Hopefully, it was only a matter of time before we caught up with him. And we had to – before his obscene urges caused another child pain.

This was 1982 and I was the detective inspector in charge of CID at the Gorbals. There had been a city-wide search for a rapist who preyed on girls as young as three; he would ask them to go into a nearby close, sometimes to look for a house with a blue door, and tell the occupant: 'Betty's had a wean.' Once he had enticed them into a secluded place, he would brutally sexually assault these young kids.

He had no mercy. He had no pity. He was a monster.

The oldest of his victims was fourteen. He put a knife to her throat and dragged her through various back courts, where he performed various sexual assaults on her. She was very lucky to escape with her life. On another occasion, this beast molested two five-year-old girls who were playing together. The descriptions received were sketchy, which is not surprising given the mental and physical condition of his young victims and the fact that he generally attacked the girls from the rear. Nevertheless, the scant information was circulated through the city and beyond.

One 24 April, a Saturday afternoon, I received a call that a young girl had been sexually attacked in a close in Langside Road. The attack was similar to the ones that had been taking place all over the city. The ten-year-old victim, extremely damaged and in severe trauma, could only supply a limited description of her assailant. This was the first attack in my area of the city but I had a feeling it would not be the last.

Looking at the pattern of his previous strikes, I was convinced that when the next attack came, it would be at a weekend. I had my troops geared up for this and made sure that I either covered weekends or was available at a moment's notice.

He struck again on the first weekend in May, this time in Govanhill, but when he tried to entice this little girl into a close she alerted two women passers-by.

I issued a force-wide alert. He had been stymied but I feared his blood would be up, meaning he would attack again that day – and my instinct was correct. An hour later, he jumped a child in Cranstonhill and yet another wee girl was put through a nightmarish ordeal.

Thanks to the little girl in Govanhill, we now had some semblance of a description. She had not been sexually assaulted, so, although shaken, was able to focus on the man and his clothing. Her description was clear and very precise for her age. At first, though, we thought that she was fantasising, as she spoke of a wee man who had green ears and spotty green hair. She also spoke of those dirty shoes but 'not the usual type of dirt'. It was difficult to understand what she meant. This little girl was very clear about what had taken place and this, combined with the description of a smallish, dark-haired man, gave us something to work on.

There was usually only a skeleton staff working at weekends in the Scottish Criminal Records Department and we wanted her to have the best possible opportunity to identify the suspect by photograph, so I made an appointment for Monday morning. Although suffering from the onset of chickenpox, she again turned out to be a real star, picking out one picture from the many we showed her.

The photograph was of Angus Robertson Sinclair, a real nasty piece of work, who had served time for the rape and murder of a seven-year-old girl in her home at St Peter's Street: only sixteen at the time, he had strangled the child with the inner tube of a bicycle tyre. For some reason, the Crown at a High Court sitting accepted his plea of culpable homicide and he served only eight years. Not enough for the snuffing out of a young life. Not nearly enough.

Since leaving prison, he'd been convicted of carrying a gun, so the photograph in police files was reasonably up to date. He looked like a good bet. I had him detained the following morning and brought to the Gorbals Office. I was there waiting for him and I immediately noticed that he had green speckles of paint in his hair and inside his ears. He was a painter and decorator. His shoes were not dirty but they were covered in paint spots. The girl's description was spot on.

He denied all knowledge of the incidents but I knew he was lying. I kept at him. I had gathered up all the available information relating to the other attacks throughout the city. My troops and I were relentless in our questioning and the interview was extremely intense, but still he wasn't saying much. Eventually, however, he began to open up slightly and I got him to speak about his present life and his interests. I took a bit of a gamble and decided to bring in his wife and talk to them together. This can be a very risky strategy, as on many occasions the spouse will immediately back up their partner. To counter this, I first spoke to the woman about his habits and his friends. She said he was very much a loner who told her very little of what he did outside the home. I let her know what her husband had been up to and this brought her onto my side. She seemed to be a very straightforward and nice woman, not what I had expected. By occupation a psychiatric nurse, she expressed horror at the crimes with which her husband was about to be charged.

When I started to talk to him in front of her, she told him to come clean regarding his actions but it took quite some time working with the two of them. I was purposely fairly brutal in my descriptions of the assaults and the woman became upset and kept telling him to admit what he had done. The strategy worked, and as I read over the charges relating to his various crimes, he began to give me short replies to each one. We got an admission to all of the crimes in such a manner that each admission corroborated the other. The procedure we followed is called the Moorov Doctrine; it relates especially to crimes of a sexual nature where there may only be a single witness who is the victim but the modus operandi of each crime is so similar they can be linked. When I charged Sinclair with the various attacks, I felt that he was only admitting to the crimes that I could prove. He certainly was not forthcoming about any others. He did not volunteer any other information other than to say, 'I've done so many I canny remember them all. I could have done 50, I just don't know.'

The stark wording of the charges in the legal documents only serves to underline the horror.

'You did . . . threaten her with a knife or similar instrument, force her to lie down, remove her clothing, lie on top of her, place your penis in her private parts and did ravish her . . .', 'seize hold of her by the shoulders, pull down her clothing and touch her on the private parts . . .', 'pull down her pants, force her to lie on the ground, threaten to kill her, insert your finger into her private parts . . .', 'insert your penis into her private parts and anus . . .'.

On and on the charges went. He said to one charge, 'Yes, that's right – that was me. I remember that wee lassie.' To another charge involving two young victims he said, 'I remember the two wee girls. That was the first time I had two of them at the one time.'

This creature made my flesh crawl – and all the while I had to make nice in order to draw as much from him as I could.

I arranged for him to stand in an identification parade at London Road Police Office, utilising the one-way mirrors available there. The victims of a number of sexual assaults studied him through the glass. Several of them were able to positively identify him as their attacker. In another room, I had Sinclair's clothes laid out and one by one the victims examined these items. Two of his jackets were picked out by a number of the girls as being those worn by the man who had assaulted them.

It was a great relief city-wide that we had caught this low-life, and I ensured that the force bulletins and telex messages regarding him specified the dangerous nature of this man and said that he must be considered for any outstanding sexual crimes. There were several unsolved murders in Strathclyde and other forces but I regret to say that the officers running these inquiries never bothered to interview Sinclair. In light of later events, perhaps they should have.

Ahead of appearing at the High Court in Edinburgh, Sinclair told his solicitor that he wished to plead guilty to the thirteen charges of rape and indecent assaults against children aged from five to fourteen between June 1978 and June 1982. He also asked that he be medically castrated, although I believe this was a ploy on his part in the hope that he would get a reduced sentence. To be honest, if he'd made this suggestion during questioning, I probably would have helped him out.

My opinion seemed to be shared by Lord Justice Cameron, who presided over the case. Sinclair did indeed plead guilty to all charges and the fact that he had requested medical castration bore no weight when it came to the sentence handed down.

Counsel appearing for Sinclair was a new man by the name of Kevin Drummond. I had never met Mr Drummond and I was very much taken aback when he approached me. Knowing other counsels, I immediately thought that he was going to be critical of the case I had put together against his client. Instead, he more or less congratulated me by saying that he wanted to meet the police officer who Sinclair had told him was one of the nicest men he had ever met. This was despite the fact, as Kevin pointed out, I was about to get him 30 years inside. Sure enough, that was the sentence handed down by the judge.

Sinclair is still locked up but his name came thundering back into the public eye a few years ago. In November 1979, the body of 17-year-old Mary Gallagher was found savagely beaten and raped in Springburn. The crime remained unsolved for over two decades, until DNA testing linked Sinclair to the crime. At 17, poor Mary was perhaps too old to fall into his usual victim profile but she was only 4 ft 11 in. tall. Sinclair was charged, tried and given a life sentence.

His next High Court appearance was less satisfactory for the Crown. Strathclyde, Lothian and Borders and Tayside Police had joined forces to set up Operation Trinity, a probe into various unsolved murders in their respective areas that might have been linked in some way. The cases in Dundee fell by the wayside, while the evidence relating to three Glasgow murders was not strong enough. However, Sinclair was implicated in a double murder in Edinburgh. In 1977, the bodies of two 17-year-old girls, Helen Scott and Christine Eadie, were found raped and strangled outside Edinburgh after drinking in the World's End pub on the Royal Mile. In 2007, Sinclair appeared in the High Court charged with these deaths. Unfortunately, due to technicalities the trial collapsed and Sinclair was released from court with a 'no case to answer' result, which means that under present law he cannot be put to court again under these charges. He continues to serve the sentences for the child rapes and the murder conviction.

To speak of the murders Sinclair may have been connected with is perhaps to lose sight of the unspeakable crimes he has been convicted of committing. Raping young kids is, to me, every bit as bad as committing murders. To him, I may have seemed one of the nicest men he'd ever met. To me, he was, and still is, an odious human being. For the record, the names of the small team of good detectives who worked on the case with me and were responsible for Sinclair's capture are Joe Woods, Graham Clark, Dennis Feeney, Tom Miller and Marie Blease. It gave us all great personal satisfaction to have put him behind bars as it meant that Sinclair has never again been free to commit horrendous crimes against vulnerable members of society.

INCEST

A case which was stunning in its depravity came to light one Saturday morning in 1984 as we detective officers were just gearing up for our usual round of visiting complainers of the previous night's crimes. The procedure was that all DOs would be allocated their share of crimes to investigate, the most serious one being given to me or to one of my detective sergeants.

A young woman, who had quite obviously been crying, was shown into the Gorbals main CID office by the bar officer. After getting her to sit down and compose herself, we asked what was troubling her. The story she began to tell immediately signalled to me the need for a policewoman member of the Female and Child Unit, a dedicated team for the protection of women and children. The policewomen attached to FACU receive a tremendous amount of training in respect of sexual crimes. Other less urgent crimes were put on hold and a detective sergeant accompanied by a FACU officer began the interview.

The young woman stayed in the area with her mother, father, one older sister and her older brother. On Friday, she had just celebrated her birthday and been out with friends for a few drinks. When she returned home, she had gone to her bed, only to be joined by her father, who demanded to have sex with her. This was not a new experience, as he had been abusing this daughter since the age of 11. But she had now decided it had to stop. We asked where her mother was while this had been taking place. She told us her mother had worked night shifts for years. She also revealed that she had three older sisters, all of whom had been abused by their father. Two had moved away, while the oldest one had returned to the family home with her two children and had apparently resumed her sexual relationship with her father. At least one of her own children had been fathered by him. There was definitely an unusual, major inquiry brewing.

Over that weekend, we had her sisters who moved away interviewed: one refused to give any type of statement about her father, although our information was that she also had a child by him; the other gave a statement alleging she had also been abused by him since her early teenage years. The older sister who had returned to the family home gave a statement of sorts but said that she could see nothing wrong with what was taking place. I spoke to the brother and asked him if he was aware of what had been taking place and he said that he used to lie in bed hearing his young sister crying as their father raped her. When I asked if he had ever abused him, he responded that it had happened only on one occasion, when none of the girls had been at home.

We charged the father with incest and lewd and libidinous behaviour and placed him before the Sheriff Court fully expecting him to be held in custody until his date of trial at the Glasgow High Court. You would expect because of the background to this case that he would be detained in custody in order to keep him away from his family. In their eternal wisdom, the Fiscal's Department agreed to a bail order and allowing him back to the family home, causing his youngest daughter to have to seek refuge elsewhere. So much for the university education lavished on budding lawyers; they should have read the definition of incest before releasing him and had some more thought about the safety and sanity of his poor daughter.

The date of the High Court trial came round and we turned up as witnesses, ready for action. The accused, however, did not appear and a warrant was granted for his immediate arrest. On our arrival at his house, his wife told us that she had not seen him for about a week. He had left telling her that he was going to 'feed the ducks' at Glasgow Green, although she thought that there might have been another reason for him visiting the River Clyde.

Sure enough, he turned up a week later floating face down in the Clyde with a large piece of concrete attached by a rope to his neck. If anybody deserved to be hanged, it was certainly him!

A sorry end to this case was that the young woman who brought the charges was ostracised by her family because she had shopped her father.

THE IBROX RAPIST

One particularly vicious case occurred just after I arrived at Govan as detective superintendent in the mid-1980s. A young woman was making her way home alone late at night when she was stopped by a man who threatened her with a knife and then dragged her onto a nearby disused railway line close to Ibrox Park. There, for a period of three to four hours, he raped and sexually abused her, before leaving her for dead after attempting to strangle her. It was a bitterly cold night and the temperature plummeted to minus six degrees. Half-naked and severely injured, she managed to drag herself to her feet and stagger over the sharp stones on the railway line. A shocked police officer walking his beat spotted the semi-clothed woman, her feet cut to ribbons, stumbling towards Paisley Road West. He called for assistance and the traumatised victim was taken to the nearby Southern General Hospital, where she was found to be suffering from hypothermia along with her injuries.

The uniformed cop who drove her to hospital had at one time been a detective. He questioned her en route and obtained a detailed description of her attacker, learning that he was about 30 years of age and had a beard.

There had been a number of unsolved rapes in the Govan area over the course of about eight years. They had not been linked or, indeed, even examined as potentially being committed by the same person. I could not understand this and took immediate steps to review all the unsolved crimes centred on a very small area between Ibrox and Paisley Road West.

The latest victim was admitted to hospital for two days and was completely distraught. Policewomen attached to FACU interviewed her at length but now she made no mention of her assailant having a beard. However, the officer who had reported this was an experienced cop and his CID background could not be ignored. Even so, in an effort to clarify things and give us the best possible chance of catching this fiend, I put the man through the wringer. He remained adamant that she had said her attacker had a beard.

Perhaps for the sake of the victims, CID bosses had decided not to go public regarding any of these other rapes. This character was a danger to all women, though, and I had no hesitation in calling a press conference the following morning. An expert from the Identification Bureau had worked with the victim in building a photofit likeness of her attacker, which can be a tremendous help in such cases, and this was issued. The photofit showed a thin-faced man, going bald but with some crinkly hair at the sides. He looked as if he was in his late twenties but had no beard.

Nicknames play a big part in Govan social life. People are often better known by them than by their real names. The publicity did the trick. Following the news bulletins and press coverage, information began to come in featuring the nickname 'Dom'. There is no doubt that sex crimes generally strike a chord with people and this particular assailant's activities were despised even by the most anti-police citizens. Soon we were getting more than a nickname. A full name, Dominic Devine, started to come through from various sources. It turned out that one of my officers had already seen him but was not confident enough to come forward and speak to me about him. This officer made a grievous error of judgement – he should have flagged the name up but didn't. I just point this out to show how easy it is to miss something that should be evident to an apparently experienced detective. Devine had been recently released from prison for the attempted rape of his sister-in-law. During his term in jail, no other rapes of the type I was looking at had occurred. I decided to take a closer look at him.

I had Devine hauled in and I faced him across the interview table. I found him very evasive but not a strong character. In appearance, he was slightly similar to the photofit. He was clean-shaven. With a little persuasion, Devine agreed to stand in an identification parade. Two victims viewed the parade – the girl from the most recent attack and a young woman who had been threatened with a hammer and raped on the waste ground that had previously been the White City dog track (now the site of Helen Street Police Office), a year or so previously.

The identification parade was held at London Road Police Office because it had the most up-to-date facilities. My witness, who had been raped only three nights previously, could not identify Devine but I put this down to the trauma of the horrific assault. However, the other victim had no problem in picking him out of the line-up. I seized the bull by the horns and had him charged at Govan. Sometimes, you take a chance and make your own luck. In this case, it worked. At midnight, I received a call at home from DI Joe Woods, a trusted colleague, telling me that Devine had requested to speak to CID. During an interview with DI Woods, he had admitted the two rapes.

The following day, I decided to push the boat out a little farther and quizzed him regarding the other rapes. He denied them all. He said he did the two but that was all. I remained unconvinced.

There were five other cases and the victims were all traced and re-interviewed. A further identification parade was set up. These crimes had taken place several years before and this can be a very tricky situation, depending on the standard of the witnesses. What struck me was that these women were still terrified to confront their attacker, even in the safety of a police office and through the screen of a one-way mirror. Devine was again identified but still refused to admit his guilt. He was locked up and I went home.

Once again, I received a call at midnight saying that Devine wished to speak with me. He said that he wanted to clear the air and admit the rest of the rapes. A voluntary statement was taken in which he admitted his guilt.

But what about the mystery of the beard? Devine himself cleared that up. It seems he did, in fact, have facial hair when he raped his last victim. Later, she recalled it but her mind blanked the memory. He shaved the beard off after the attack and when she saw him in the line-up she did not identify him. Subconsciously, she knew he had a beard, so she did not recognise him without it. During the inquiry, photos were obtained showing his bearded features. One thing that is always taught to police officers is that, in the case of serious assault or rape, the quicker the reaction of the victim can be assessed and a statement taken, the better. An early statement will often be a very telling factor in the ensuing investigation. In this case, the cop who took the first description had obtained one that was accurate and true.

Dominic Devine pleaded guilty on all counts and received a sentence of 14 years at the High Court in Glasgow.

The Boss

Although I had thoroughly enjoyed my seven busy years as a detective inspector at the Gorbals, I was getting extremely fed up, not with the job but with the injustice of the personnel system: continually seeing other officers being promoted ahead of me meant that I was seriously considering leaving the force. My luck changed, however, and I was promoted to detective chief inspector in the Serious Crime Squad. Although I say that my luck changed, it had nothing to do with luck. The bosses simply required someone who was not afraid to lock up neds and knew how to do it properly. I like to think I fitted the profile – and there are a number of neds who might agree.

The job of DCI in a Serious Crime Squad staffed with good detectives was one I had always dreamed of. Like the old Flying Squad, each division was required to provide its quota of officers to man the squad. Theoretically, it should have been the best and the brightest who were recommended for secondment or transfer to the squad. As with the Flying Squad, though, sometimes, bosses did not want to lose their best officers, so they would compromise and send those of a lesser calibre. I found myself second in command of a mixed bag. However, I was very lucky to have alongside me a great friend and good working partner, Superintendent Jimmy Young. My method of leadership was from the front and it remained that way. I might not always have been backed up by those above or around me but I am pleased to say my system worked, more often than not.

After a short seven months as number two, I was again promoted, this time within the squad. In fact, Jimmy was promoted to chief superintendent in charge of the Support Unit and I was to become the head of the Serious Crime Squad. I was totally taken by surprise but quite delighted. I saw this as being the ideal position from which to sort out major criminals and influence future CID policy.

A CASE FOR HOLMES

At about 11 p.m. on a Thursday night in 1986, someone entered a bedroom in a housing estate on the edge of Dumbarton with a rock in his hand and beat the 50-year-old female resident to death. The killer then covered the victim's face and raped her. After the murder and necrophilia, he set fire to the house in an effort to cover up his actions.

It was a particularly brutal and nasty crime, and a major inquiry was immediately instigated at Dumbarton Police Office, the divisional headquarters in that area. The following day, I reported as usual to my post in force headquarters and was told about the Dumbarton murder. It was brought to the Serious Crime Squad's attention because Strathclyde Police, under the redoubtable leadership of Chief Constable Andrew Sloan, had signed up for an extremely expensive new system – the Home Office Large Major Enquiry System (HOLMES), which utilised a computer-driven incident-room system. HOLMES had never before been used in

Scotland and so Sloan wanted his force to be the first to try it out.

The HOLMES system was inaugurated in response to the intense criticism of flawed police procedure in the Yorkshire Ripper case: during that long hunt, there was a vast amount of duplication of intelligence, information not picked up and crucial evidence allowed to slip through the net. The result was that Peter Sutcliffe got away with his heinous crimes for years.

I had already dispatched some of my Serious Crime Squad detective officers to assist at Dumbarton when I was summoned to my assistant chief constable's office to be told that I had to take over the inquiry. This was tricky on two fronts – first, telling the local DCI that I was taking charge in his division on his inquiry and, second, taking responsibility for running the first HOLMES murder inquiry in Scotland. I needn't have worried on the first count. The DCI was delighted to hand over the reins, partly because he had practically never seen a computer before, never mind the full HOLMES set-up, but also because he had detectives on his team who had never worked on a major inquiry, let alone a murder as horrific as this. I had been trained on the new system and had already figured the proper way to use it without allowing the computer whizzkids to tie a learner like me in knots.

My approach was to work HOLMES to the fullest while at the same time never sidelining tried and tested means. The tried and tested means were, of course, thorough, old-fashioned detective work involving excellent police officers with extensive experience in dealing with major crimes, and who knew how I liked things dealt with. In this way, many difficult and awkward cases were solved.

In this particular inquiry, it was also crucial to incorporate good local officers into the hub of the investigation. Local knowledge is vitally important. On the night of the murder, a shift inspector told a senior officer that a local youth had seen the blaze and gone into the house, apparently to see if he could give assistance to the woman. The youth said that he had been overcome by smoke and so was unable to help her. The shift inspector was not happy with his story and said as much to the senior officer. However, this did not seem to be taken on board and instead the local press were told that the lad had acted like a hero in trying to enter the blazing building.

When my team started to dig into the case, we found that this youth already knew the victim. Witnesses were traced who had seen him lurking in bushes nearby, seemingly watching the fire take hold. This was immediately before the supposed rescue attempt, which was beginning to look like a clumsy ruse to cover the fact that he had already been in the house. He said he had not reached the victim but had probably left his fingerprints. I therefore issued instructions that the clothing he had been wearing that night was to be sent to the Forensic Lab for examination.

Obviously, all other apects of the inquiry were continuing, such as examination of the locus and gathering background information. I also liaised with fire chiefs, whom I found to be first class in their professionalism and input, inasmuch as they removed all that they could from the bedroom and reconstructed it in the gym hall of the police office where I had set up my Inquiry Room. This reconstruction was rather grisly, as many of the items were not only blackened and reeked of smoke but were also heavily bloodstained, and it brought a sense of realism to the rather sterile atmosphere of the HOLMES room. Any detectives who perhaps lost sight of what we were there for only had to go to that corner of the gym to remind themselves that a woman had died.

I was waiting with bated breath for the forensic report. I had a feeling that it would be crucial to this inquiry, and indeed it was. Examination of the youth's clothes yielded the information that they were spattered with the victim's blood. At this stage, I had not interviewed him myself, although other officers had at the time of the incident. It was clearly time I had a wee word with him. I sent a team of officers to his home to collect him and bring him to Dumbarton Police Office. It then took a very short time to get him to admit that he had committed the rape and murder. He elected to give a voluntary statement. He said that he had met the unfortunate victim at a church meeting and had been in her house before, so he was aware that she lived alone. That night, he had decided that he would visit her to satisfy his lustful needs.

I was sure that the murder was no accident. It seemed obvious to me that he had planned the attack, because he had carried a large stone into this lady's home and used it to batter her to death.

In my opinion, the case could have been solved on the night it happened if the excellent information given by the shift inspector had been listened to. Laurie Wilson had worked with me in the Serious Crime Squad and I knew him to be a sharp cop. Instead, it took the best part of a week and many man-hours, costing the force a small fortune.

In court, the ned received a life sentence, which was no more than he deserved.

IN HARM'S WAY

By the time I was put in charge of the Serious Crime Squad, it had dramatically increased in size. Chief Constable Sir Patrick Hamill had obviously realised its worth to the force. The commitment of Serious Crime Squad officers sometimes put them in situations of some peril.

One of the teams was dealing with a series of armed robberies at pubs just as they were about to open. This was in the days when pubs had to close in the afternoon before opening again at 5 p.m. The raids were taking place either mid-morning or late afternoon, just before opening time. The robbers kept a watch on certain premises waiting for the keyholder to turn up, then pounced as the door was opened and the alarm switched off. They would bundle the pub staff into the premises, throw them onto the floor and threaten them with guns until they agreed to open the safe, if there was one. Their hands and feet were secured with plastic garden ties and tape was plastered over their mouths before the robbers legged it with whatever cash they had found. There were always two robbers involved and they always got clean away.

There had been a spate of these crimes in and around the city centre and pub owners were on full alert for anything unusual. Meanwhile, one of the squad detective sergeants, Les Darling, had managed to gain information regarding the activities of two suspects who stayed in the East End of the city.

One weekend, I had just returned from a holiday break when I was contacted at home and told that a large team of my men were actively engaged that Sunday keeping tabs on a group thought to be involved in the pub robberies. A full surveillance team had been deployed with a backup team of armed officers. The surveillance unit was watching the homes of the suspects, waiting for them to make a move. That afternoon, a black Hackney cab arrived with a middle-aged woman at the wheel and a younger woman in the back. The cab idled in the street until two men came out of the house and climbed in. One of the men was carrying a large holdall.

The taxi began to head towards the city centre, still monitored by the surveillance officers, while the armed team kept their distance, remaining in touch with one another by radio. The targets drove along the side of the River Clyde then turned towards Charing Cross. In North Street, the taxi drew to a halt. There were several public houses in the immediate vicinity, one of them being the Avalon Bar in Kent Road. The men left the cab, the taller of the two carrying the holdall. The cab moved a short distance away and waited – still with the two females on board.

The men began knocking at the door of the Avalon, obviously hoping that maybe one of the staff was still on the premises, but there was no one in the pub. The men lingered outside. To the watching officers, it was obvious they were working out the target for their next robbery. The men returned to the taxi, which began driving towards Charing Cross.

The roads were fairly quiet and the officer in charge of the operation decided that he had sufficient grounds to merit a 'pull' (stop the taxi and interview its occupants). As it neared a set of traffic lights, police vehicles screamed to a halt in front and behind, blocking it in. Officers piled out of the cars and moved towards the cab. Then someone spotted one of the rear windows rolling down and the twin barrels of a shotgun pointed directly at them. A warning was yelled and the detectives ducked for cover behind their vehicle, screaming into their radios for armed backup. The firearms detectives were not far away and they roared up within seconds. One officer, Detective Constable George Adair, approached the nearside of the taxi while his partner, Detective Sergeant Les Darling, covered the offside of the vehicle, both shouting the mantra, 'Armed police officers! Put your weapon down! Armed police officers! Put your weapon down!'

The man took no notice and continued to brandish the shotgun through the window at the cops. DC Adair pulled open the back door, noticed the second man on the squab seat nearest to him, but kept his main focus on the man with the shotgun, who was still leaning out of the window. Hearing the door opening, the gunman began to swivel round. George, still shouting that he was a police officer, fired once. The bullet struck the man on the backside and propelled him out of the opposite door of the taxi. His weapon clattered to the ground as he sprawled into the street. Meanwhile, DC Adair turned his attention to the second man, who was reaching into his jacket. George pointed his gun at him and warned, 'Make a move and I'll blow your fucking head off.' Not textbook perhaps but certainly effective. The ned quickly removed his hand. George reached under the man's jacket and plucked a handgun from a shoulder holster. These robbers had certainly come prepared.

The taxi was now completely surrounded by other officers, some with weapons unholstered, and the rest of the gang was dragged from the vehicle and arrested. An ambulance was called and the wounded ned was taken to Glasgow Royal Infirmary. The bullet had struck him on a fleshy part of his anatomy and then travelled up his back, eventually coming to rest at his shoulder. It was successfully removed. He was lucky. Bullets can do funny things in the body and this one could easily have hit a vital organ.

I was at home while all of this was taking place and the first garbled message I received was that one of my officers had been shot. I was on my way to my car to attend when I received a further message that it was the ned who had been shot. I still, of course, decided to attend but in a far more relaxed manner and at a slower speed.

Kenneth Ross, the wounded man, was an ex-soldier who had served two terms in Northern Ireland and was obviously not a person to be trifled with when it came to wielding a gun. The other ned was simply his accomplice. The taxi provided terrific cover for the raiders. Who would suspect the occupants of a taxi when an armed robbery had taken place?

Whenever a firearm is discharged by a police officer, procedure dictates immediate steps that must be taken by senior officers. The cops involved in the incident must be separated and interviewed by a senior ranking officer. Their guns are taken away and submitted for forensic testing. All of this helps to ensure that everything is above board. In this instance, it was amazing how some senior detectives immediately looked upon the officers concerned as criminals who were somehow to blame for the incident. This led to a confrontation between me and another officer of equal rank who was heard to be running about in Baird Street Police Office openly declaring that if any officers were at fault, he would have them. This was before he was aware of the complete circumstances surrounding the arrests. In any event, he drafted in a number of detective inspectors and insisted that the teams involved in the arrests be split up and interviewed separately by two ranking officers each. I had no problem with this – it was the correct procedure – but I did have a problem with his attitude, as it seemed to me that he was determined to blame one of my men rather than objectively view the whole set of circumstances. The discussion between the two of us became so heated that he eventually left the building.

The gang appeared at the High Court and received various sentences for their involvement in the series of robberies. Kenneth Ross was charged with 16 counts of armed robbery and the attempted murder of Detective Sergeant Les Darling and Detective Constable John Mooney.

This was a tremendous result for the Serious Crime Squad but it was soured by the reaction to the use of the firearms. George Adair did not even receive a commendation for the sterling work he did that day. In fact, at a later meeting I attended to discuss the ongoing situation regarding firearms, an assistant chief constable criticised George for, as the assistant chief constable so delicately put it, using the 'F' word while arresting two armed robbers. I doubt if this particular officer had ever seen an angry man in his career. He went on to suggest that it would probably be wise to issue handguns to dog-handlers. I tried to explain that the present method of training recommended a two-handed grip when using side arms and it would evidently be rather awkward controlling a large Alsatian dog while aiming a pistol in a fraught situation. I felt that this exchange showed how little the ACC knew of that type of real police work and how little I knew of being circumspect. I was later informed by internal mail that my presence would not be required at the next meeting. That suited me. Talking policy around a table was never my idea of catching neds anyway.

I remained in charge of the squad for another year or so before reshuffles took place above me that dictated that I was to be moved from the job that I felt I was made for. This has always been a source of annoyance to me, as it was not done purely for sound operational reasons. However, every cloud has a silver lining. When I took over the CID of 'G' Division, based in Govan, I didn't realise this was going to be another turning point in my career: I was about to have the great opportunity to prove that I had a talent for running major inquiries and for catching really bad neds.

It was also at Govan that I met a detective constable called Katie, who turned out to be my saviour as far as my private life was concerned. I was instantly impressed by everything about her, especially her sense of humour. Shortly after I arrived at Govan, she was transferred to the Drug Squad. Several years later, she became my third wife – as she says, I've got a fondness for wedding cake.

In Govan, I found myself in charge of the CID in one of the hardest areas within Strathclyde, if not Scotland, and it soon became clear that this was the worst division crime-wise. It had been well chosen by the hierarchy at headquarters for me. While I was there, there were 15 divisions in the force and mine accounted for nearly 20 per cent of all murders. Someone upstairs probably thought they were doing me a bad turn by sending me there but they were wrong. I like to be challenged and 'G' Division did that, every single day.

Govan

OPERATION BUCKFAST

Govan Division sprawls over a huge part of Glasgow's south side, taking in areas of varying social and ethnic backgrounds. The division was the most violent in Scotland at the time I moved there – and 'G' Division had more than its fair share of murders and attempted murders to contend with. Manpower was always stretched. As the senior CID officer, I was in charge of these major inquiries and was always very busy, either starting up a new inquiry or tidying up an old one. I had an excellent team of detectives who had become most skilful in dealing with major investigations.

The drugs situation was the most prevalent cause of crime. This was usually dealt with at street level by uniformed and plain-clothes cops, and was a very dirty and thankless job. The Drug Squad, which operated out of force headquarters, was always on hand should they be required for larger operations. The officers in the squad were hard-working cops who were always on the go, as by the late '80s the drugs problem was pretty rife throughout the region. Nowadays, each division has its own drugs team to focus on local issues and liaise with the main Drug Squad whenever necessary.

As it happened, I was between murder inquiries when two uniformed officers – Sergeant Angus McIvor and a constable – arrived at my office to report that there was an increasing problem regarding the trading of heroin in an area known locally as 'the Wine Alley'.

There have been many stories written about the Wine Alley, a very compact housing scheme of only a few streets, originally named Moorpark. Many families had migrated here from the Gorbals during the housing regeneration of the mid-twentieth-century and they had brought their drinking habits with them. The type of wine referred to in the area's nickname is not a cheeky little Beaujolais or Châteauneuf-du-Pape but the Four Crown or Buckfast tonic wine variety. I have never discovered what ailments Buckfast cures but, having spoken to quite a few prisoners who have partaken of this beverage, I know that bad breath is certainly not one of them. It was the prevalence of this wine that gave the resulting drugs operation its name – 'Operation Buckfast'.

Apparently, the alley's drug scene really took off thanks to an older ned called Eddie Burnside who lived there and ran a team of younger neds throughout the Govan area from his own close. The layout suited his endeavours. There were only two ways in and out of the Wine Alley, which meant Burnside's young watchers could easily spot any police activity. There was no point in bursting into the alley heavy-handed in order to scoop up the drug users hanging about, as the dealers themselves would have been long gone. However, there were quite a few empty houses near to where the activity was happening and Sergeant McIvor and his young colleague volunteered to try to find one that could be used as an observation post. We wanted to video and record the drug deals, so whatever spot they found would have to put them very close to the action. This was not only a tricky proposition but also a dangerous one – two plain-clothes cops caught in an empty house in this area were on a hiding to nothing. They went in and out of their observation post during the hours of darkness, leading to long, stressful and tiring shifts.

It was a dicey strategy but deemed worth the risk. We managed to obtain keys to an appropriate house but getting our two cops in and out was going to be difficult, so this had to be achieved at times when the neds weren't about. This meant that the two officers were doing something close to 18-hour shifts in the grubbiest and most dangerous of conditions.

Just across from the Wine Alley are several blocks of council high flats known as Iona Court. At this time, there were a number of empty flats, especially on the highest floors. One, on the eighth floor, was obtained for a second observation post. I procured the services of our photographic branch in order to set up long-distance video and stills cameras plus a professional cameraman in order to record the happenings at the front of Burnside's close.

I had learned that there was a daily circus performed there. Burnside, who stayed on the top floor three storeys up, would hang out of his window and throw out what appeared to be small paper deals of 'smack', or heroin, and entertain himself with the sight of the poor users scrabbling and fighting one another for them. We wanted to identify which users were there on more or less every occasion. All the regular customers were nabbed as they left the Alley and taken to Govan Police Office, where we learned more of Burnside's tricks.

One of his most frequent users had at one time been a police officer. He had been identified as an addict while still on the job and this had led to his dismissal from the force. He was one of the regulars grabbed up and interviewed. The statement he gave was very specific regarding the way in which Burnside distributed his drugs and the names of his lieutenants, who were also going to be targeted in this operation. Burnside was most sadistic in his practice of throwing the 'deals' out of the window: most of the wraps contained nothing. He used to have a great laugh at the antics of his clients scrambling about in the dirt.

Thanks to the work in Sergeant McIvor's post and the high vantage point of the flat, we learned a great deal about the comings and goings at Burnside's headquarters, both of people and vehicles, the latter of which are, of course, easily traceable. One in particular was a fairly new, small car, which we learned was owned by a local car-hire firm. The company had no clue what use their car was being put to and could not have been more helpful. The ned, whom they named as a regular customer, was a known dealer. In addition to hiring small cars, they told us that he also rented a larger vehicle about twice a month. They knew from the recorded mileage that he took this vehicle on longer trips and assumed that whatever business he was in took him further afield. More importantly, he was due to take one away in two days' time.

The car-hire firm was not wrong about their customer's business taking him further afield. It was obviously business, but not legitimate business. His journey would normally be something in the region of 600 miles, with the car returned the following day. To us, this suggested a trip to Liverpool or Manchester to collect a consignment of drugs. He'd hit on a good ploy. By using a different car on each of his drug collections, he ensured the registration number was always different – perhaps an expensive way of running his business but pretty anonymous and it had kept him free of long jail sentences. So far, at any rate.

Burnside, on the other hand, was far more blasé and obviously thought that in his little Wine Alley enclave he was untouchable. It proved very simple for the officers keeping him under observation to gather registration numbers used by him and his gang and go on to track their movements. We knew he always went team-handed when collecting a consignment, which fitted his profile of being something of a bully and, in Glasgow parlance, a bit of a chancer or craw – in other words, not terribly brave.

I now had two scenarios running side by side. We had targeted Burnside originally and gleaned a good deal of information regarding his operation. As a bit of a bonus, we also had the lead on the car-renting ned. For the next two days, I kept the observation posts up and running, waiting for the movements suggesting that there might be runs down to England to collect their supplies of heroin.

On the third day, my team was told that the car hirer was about to collect a bigger vehicle. The young woman who worked at the car-hire firm was quite taken by the attention she was receiving from a young detective officer and was supplying first-class information. It looked as if a run was in the offing. The Drug Squad surveillance team was alerted, as they had been taking a keen interest in the operation and were ready to assist in following the suspects if needed. On the afternoon of that day, the car hirer collected his bigger car and made for the M8 motorway almost straight away. Detectives followed and he headed for the M74 southwards. Part of the operation seemed to be taking shape. Many things not only can – but do – go wrong and when you are waiting to be updated by surveillance officers it can be a bit nerve-racking. But I have been on surveillance teams and I know it is far worse for them. Trust is necessary on both sides and the last thing that officers on a plot need is for some nervy boss to be looking for updates every five minutes.

I still had the Burnside situation cooking away merrily. I thought we would be able to relax until we heard from the officers who had headed down south on the follow. However, as I have said, not everything goes the way that you hope it will. Just before 5 p.m., things started to happen at the Burnside close. One of his lieutenants drew up outside in his car, then Burnside and another three of his gang climbed in. I already had a further team of Drug Squad surveillance officers standing by and passed the information to them that our boy was on the move and probably heading down south.

The M74 was pretty busy that day, with drug dealers and a

collection of Drug Squad officers all travelling to England. Things were moving fast – so fast that the detective inspector in charge of the second convoy was abandoned at a service area the suspects had drawn into. He took the opportunity to go to the toilet and was left, high and dry, when the convoy unexpectedly took off again. The team returned to collect him some hours later. I have never been able to make up my mind if they had left him behind on purpose. He never lived it down afterwards.

For my team and me back at Govan, it was a waiting game. I learned that the car hirer had indeed headed for Liverpool, where he was seen going to a house and then leaving in a very short space of time. He headed back northwards to the M6, seemingly Scotland-bound. My instructions to my teams had been for them to follow and we would make the hit as near home as possible. They kept their distance but did not lose sight of him.

Just before midnight, the first suspect arrived back in Govan, coming off the M8 at Helen Street. As he approached the first set of traffic lights, the surveillance officers decided to take him. As they surrounded the car, his driver's door was wrenched open by a young Drug Squad policewoman. He panicked and grabbed a plastic bag containing the drugs, clearly intending to throw them from the car. The young policewoman immediately grabbed hold of his testicles and was heard to instruct him loudly in her cut-glass accent, 'Let go of the smack, son, and I'll let go of your balls.' He hastily did as he was told.

He was handed over to my officers, who duly locked him up. The street value of the smack he had brought from Liverpool to sell to the local addicts was around £50,000. He later went to the High Court in Glasgow and received a guilty verdict and eight years' imprisonment.

The Drug Squad team who had followed him back turned tail and headed south again to assist the second team. We knew from radio updates that the Burnside vehicle had gone into a very dodgy area of

Liverpool and it had not been possible to follow closely to the neds'
pick-up point. The surveillance team did their usual excellent job
and covered all exit points and routes to the motorway. Shortly after
midnight, the vehicle was spotted heading north on the motorway. It
appeared that there was only one occupant. Speculation ensued as to
what had become of the others. Had they stayed in Liverpool for the
night? Or was this not a drugs run at all but some kind of pleasure
trip for the rest of them? It was decided to stay with the vehicle,
which continued north towards Scotland by the shortest route – M6
to M74 then onto the M8 and over the Kingston Bridge.

I was receiving a running commentary throughout and was asked
at this stage whether they should stop the vehicle. I instructed them to
follow it into Govan. Then the pursuing cops had a bit of a surprise.
Everything had seemed to be under control until suddenly another
four heads popped up in the target vehicle. Nobody realised that the
others had been having a snooze on the way up the road to Glasgow.

It is very different stopping a car containing one suspect, as
opposed to one containing a nasty team, especially if it is a group of
drug dealers transporting their gear. There was some debate now over
the best way to intercept them. As it turned out, not one but two
phoney road accidents were set up on the slip roads to Govan that the
gang would be likely to use. One of these staged accidents slowed the
gang's progress considerably at the Ibrox cut-off, allowing the Drug
Squad officers to swoop on the target vehicle.

Finding themselves surrounded by a mob of shouting police officers,
the neds immediately locked all doors on the car but that did them no
good at all. A swift swing of a sturdy baton wielded by a Drug Squad
officer smashed the front window and all of the suspects were hauled
out of the car. They were found to be in possession of a large sum of
money and an even larger amount of heroin. The presence of cash
obviously suggested that had more drugs been available, they would
have been bought. As it was, the estimated value of the drugs found
on Burnside and his cohorts was in the region of £150,000. The cells

at Govan were filling up nicely. This had been a very productive day for the police.

Burnside received a 12-year prison sentence at Glasgow High Court. His cohorts got six to eight years' imprisonment.

After that result, a number of letters arrived for me, apparently from residents of the Wine Alley although none of them were signed, thanking the police for what had been done to make their daily lives a bit easier. These responses were much appreciated by all the officers who had been involved. I put recommendations to the Chief Constable that the two local uniformed officers, Sergeant McIvor and his colleague, should receive proper recognition for their role in bringing the gang to justice.

THE SIEGE OF BROOMLOAN COURT

One morning in May 1988, I was having my first cup of coffee when one of my sergeants came bursting into my room in a high state of hysteria shouting, 'Boss, that's the ball up the slates now', which I took to mean that there was some type of trouble brewing.

I was not used to my seasoned sergeants behaving in such a manner, so after giving him a pat on the head and a lump of sugar to calm him down, I got him to explain himself. He had just taken a call from the manager of Security Express, a company based in nearby Broomloan Road near to Ibrox Park. The manager, Gordon Slater, said that he had spotted something not quite right about the demeanour of one of his long-term employees, John Burke, who was normally very steady and reliable. A security company has to be sensitive to the fact that their workers are responsible for the transfer of large sums of cash and Mr Slater had been very sharp in spotting that something was wrong. He sat Burke down in his office and spoke to him. The story he told prompted the call to the police.

It seemed that the previous evening, three men had invaded Burke's home in Maryhill. Brandishing guns, knives and a cut-throat razor, they had taken the entire family captive – his wife, his four sons (two of them also employees of the firm), his daughter-in-law and a young child. Their plan was to use the family as hostages to force their father to steal money from his employer.

My sergeant was correct. The ball was up on the slates and it was up to the police to get it down.

My divisional commander was Willie Marshall, the best divisional boss I've ever worked for, and he was my first call. I then alerted headquarters. Both calls were made in double-quick time and I headed to the premises of Security Express. The building was only five minutes away, so I walked rather than take a car in case the gang was keeping the place under observation, and it also gave me thinking time. Mr Burke told me that the gang had arrived around midnight. They burst in waving their weapons and completely terrorised the family. One of his sons was battered on the head with the butt of a sawn-off shotgun before they were all handcuffed and their eyes covered with sticky tape. The thugs continued to scream threats at them to keep them in line.

Burke was then told by the gang that his family would remain as hostages while he went to work the next day and collected £150,000 during his tour of duty. He was to hand over the cash as the ransom for his family. The stipulation was that this money had to be paid by midday. Burke told me the proposed location of the handover.

Two of the neds took some of the family away by car. The rest, including Burke, were left in the house with the third ned, who continued to behave like a maniac. A short time later, the car reappeared and the rest of the hostages were bundled into it, leaving Burke in a state of complete shock, wondering what he could best do to save his family. The gang had warned him what would happen to his loved ones if he even thought about talking to the police. The poor man was beside himself with worry for the rest of the night, as he did not know where his family had been taken or how they were being treated.

It was in this state – sick with worry, groggy through lack of sleep – that he turned up for work. He did not know what the best course of action was. He did not know how to handle the situation and was extremely relieved when the sharp-eyed Mr Slater spoke to him.

I arranged for several of my officers, headed by a detective inspector, to quietly join me at the security company offices. My idea was to monitor all incoming calls, in case any were from the gang. In cases such as this, you have to think in several different directions at the same time. Everything had to be considered. One possible scenario was that John Burke and his family, two of whom worked for the same company, knowing the large amounts of cash being transported every day, had set this up.

The interview with John Burke was crucial to my assessment of the situation. The man was in a high state of anxiety but he would have been in any case, no matter what his involvement. I had to watch him closely during our talk in order to gauge his reaction to questions and decide if he had the bottle to be involved in such a plot. However, I believed his story and was of the firm opinion that we did indeed have a hostage situation on our hands. Not everyone agreed. Detective Chief Superintendent John Orr arrived from headquarters to assess what was a highly unusual and volatile situation. We were also under the gun with regards to time. It was now 8.30 a.m. and the gang had given Mr Burke a noon deadline. As DCS Orr and I walked back to the police office from the security firm, he remarked that he did not believe Burke. I replied, 'Whatever the truth is, someone will be appearing at the High Court.' By this time I had made up my mind that he was a decent man and was not capable of carrying out such a charade. Mr Orr then headed back to headquarters, telling me that should I need any further assistance he could be reached there.

I then had to get my thinking cap on and decide on the best, quickest and safest way to solve this dilemma. My staff was still *in situ* at the Security Express premises and I was happy with the cover in place there. Much more needed to be done and could not be done by my officers alone, so I called in the assistance of the Serious Crime Squad, requesting they be armed and ready for action. My second-in-command, Chief Inspector Harry Bell, was a hugely competent and dependable cop. As things turned out, it was just as well.

Burke had told me that the drop-off point for the money was to be in Craigton Cemetery just off Shieldhall Road. There he would see the small red car used to ferry his family from his home. He had to follow this car into the cemetery. We knew the handover was to take place at noon but we had no idea what kind of surveillance the gang would carry out. We knew three men had snatched the family but had no way of knowing if there were more involved. I called in specialist police surveillance units to cover all points around the Security Express depot. I had officers inside the building and now the outside was covered. My plan, which I had discussed with the team, was to have Burke go on his usual route as if he was collecting cash from various companies as normal. Burke and Slater readily agreed to this. They left everything in my hands and the company was totally cooperative.

Harry Bell and DS John Boyd made their way on foot to the firm's premises, where they were kitted out in Security Express uniforms. There was one small difference between them and normal security men – they were both armed. This gang had already waved a shotgun and blades around. They had brutally battered one of Burke's sons. We were not taking any chances. Harry was detailed to drive the vehicle, with Burke in the passenger seat and John secreted in the back of the van with two other armed officers and a police radio so that he could remain in constant contact with me. In addition, police surveillance units would shadow the van. I had instructed that the van should follow its normal route. Each firm on this route had been contacted and told not to give any cash to the guards; we used the cover story that this was a test exercise and that their cash would be collected later that day. I had no intention of giving money to the gang!

All of these precautions and arrangements were made with one eye on the clock, for the noon deadline was approaching. Members of the Serious Crime Squad had already staked out the cemetery and were feeding information back to me constantly. I had requested that the Police Armed Response Unit be on standby. Then the radio crackled with the news from the squad officers at the cemetery that there was a young man loitering near to the gates. He was identified as a Raymond Graham, a known face in Govan.

After what seemed like an age, John Boyd's laid-back tones were heard on the police radio. They were in Shieldhall Road and could see the red car parked at the cemetery entrance. The driver had signalled them to follow him into the graveyard. The other officers on the ground were all warned not to make a move until the gang made full contact. Once the van entered the cemetery, detectives grabbed Raymond Graham and huckled him into a nearby vehicle. One down, two to go!

Inside the cemetery, the ned in the car directed the security van to halt. He then left his car and approached the van. Nerves were jumping in the cab because they fully expected him to be armed. John Burke must have been beside himself as he faced one of the men responsible for terrorising his family. Fortunately, the man approached Harry's side of the van. Taking no chances, Harry leapt out at him ready for a struggle but the ned took to his heels. Serious Crime Squad officers, guns in hand, rose like phantoms from behind gravestones and took off after him. He dodged between the graves but he was rugby-tackled by one athletic officer, brought to the ground and rather roughly subdued. He was searched but was found not be armed.

His name was Sean Garty and, like Raymond Graham, was a well-known Govan crook. This was slightly surprising, because I half-expected the gang to be from the north side of the city where the Burkes lived.

Raymond Graham was the brother of an escaped prisoner and local desperado, Danny 'Scarface' Graham, who had been on the run for some time having escaped from prison and was suspected of being responsible for a number of bank robberies. This bit of news obviously placed him in the frame as the other abductor.

We still had not found the Burke family and my main priority was to interview Garty and Graham to find out where they were. I had Garty taken to the detective sergeants' room in Govan Police Office, where I intended to interview him along with Harry Bell.

The Burke family, ranging from a lady in her late fifties to a child of two years, had now been held for some fourteen hours, under what conditions it was hard to imagine. Given their ages and considering they probably were in the hands of Danny Graham, it was essential to locate them quickly. I asked Garty where they were but he refused to burst. I noticed that he kept looking at the clock on the wall of the sergeant's room and I saw that he was getting very fidgety as the time grew closer to 1 p.m. I guessed that if Danny Graham did not hear from his pals soon, then he might do something really stupid. I decided to take a gamble. I spelled out the charges Garty was about to face but he simply shrugged – until I told him that they would also include one of murder. This provoked a reaction from him.

'We've no killed anyone,' he said.

I asked, 'Did you know the kid you snatched was diabetic?' I paused to let this sink in, and then added for emphasis, just in case he didn't understand, 'She should've had an insulin injection this morning. Without it, she's likely to die. And that would be murder.'

It sank in then and he folded like a pack of cards. A little white lie had done the trick – the child was not diabetic but the scare was enough for Garty to spill his guts as to the location of the family. It turned out that they were being held in a derelict flat almost opposite the Security Express offices on the eighth floor of Broomloan Court. Garty stated that they had broken into an empty house, which was being used as the stronghold. The wheel had turned full circle regarding the location of the crime. It had begun on the north side of the city but had landed squarely back in my lap in Govan. Our first action was to have the block of flats contained and ensure that all the residents came to no harm. Easier said than done, considering that there were six houses on each floor, nineteen floors in total.

My divisional commander, Willie Marshall, accompanied by Superintendent Alistair Kilgour, took on this massive containment task, swiftly orchestrating it by utilising every available officer, as well as calling in outside help from the Serious Crime Squad, the Firearms Unit and the Dog Branch. They were instructed to divert every member of the public who tried to enter the flats to a nearby school, where they were kept out of harm's way. Cordons were set up around the building and snipers were placed on the surrounding high flats as we attempted to positively identify the house concerned. There were a number of derelict flats on the floor specified by Garty but only one contained an armed and dangerous gunman holding a group of terrified hostages. We were keenly aware that time was of the essence. It had been quite a while since his accomplices had left to make the pick-up; they had not returned and in Danny Graham's mind there could be only two reasons for this – either Burke had double-crossed them and alerted the law, or his pals had double-crossed him and had made off with the pay-off. Either way, it placed the prisoners in a very dangerous situation.

The building was searched systematically but the job was enormous. Officers swarmed into the block, moving floor by floor above and below the eighth level, clearing the area of as many civilians as possible. Chief Inspector Bob Gordon, affectionately known as 'Guns Gordon', was in charge of the elite Firearms Unit and together he and I had to devise a plan for safe entry. We wanted no one hurt that day, not the hostages, not the police, not even the ned with the gun.

I was receiving updates from various officers who were examining the windows with binoculars and rifle scopes. One officer in a sniper's position called in to report that he could see a young man at an eighth floor window who appeared to be holding something metallic in his hand, which could have been a gun. The officer was requesting permission to fire. Thankfully, I refused this request; it later turned out that the person at the window was, in fact, one of the hostages showing the handcuffs that he was still wearing. Everyone was very tense but at least this sighting had positively identified the flat.

One big problem was that there were about three different types of radio in use by the various units involved, each operating on their own frequency. It was my job to keep complete control of them all and ensure that nobody went off at half-cock. All the while, I was continually receiving calls from headquarters asking for updates. They wanted to know what was going on but were keeping their distance from the actual decision-making and action-taking.

We had reached the stage where we were ready to storm the house; this was to be carried out by the Firearms Unit led by Bob Gordon. I decided that I would accompany them into the house, as the incident was reaching a crucial stage and had to be dealt with in a most careful manner. There were young men in this house who could well have been mistaken for criminals – and such a mistake could prove tragic.

We were in the stairwell, about to approach the door, when Guns suggested that it would be a good idea to have a police dog and handler enter the house first. I was starting to lose patience but I agreed and a dog was sent for. When the handler arrived and was told what was required of him, his immediate reaction was that his dog needed the toilet and would have to go back down all eight floors and outside to a nice wee area of grass so that he could perform his duty. I think that it was the handler whose bowels were loose. I chased him and his dog back downstairs.

We could now hear shouting and screaming coming from inside the flat and realised that this was the hostages calling for help. We yelled through the door and were told that Graham had left them on their own shortly before our arrival. On entering, we found the family still in a state of terror. The men were still handcuffed. They all had to be calmed and told they were safe. In the house, we found a bag containing a sawn-off shotgun, a handgun and a cut-throat razor. The family, apart from being extremely upset, appeared in reasonably good health, although one of the young men had a deep laceration on his forehead, the result of the blow from the shotgun butt the night before.

A fleet of ambulances were on standby to ferry them to hospital. Staff from the Female and Child Unit accompanied the women to the Southern General Hospital for treatment. Needless to say, John Burke, who had remained at Govan Police during the freeing of his family, was totally delighted with the outcome. This man had been a tower of strength throughout his ordeal and Harry Bell, who was with him in the van, could not speak highly enough of his courage and composure.

We were not finished. Graham was still was on the loose. I believed he was still somewhere within the block of flats, because we knew what he looked like and with police all around there was no way he could have escaped without being spotted. In consultation with Willie Marshall and Alistair Kilgour, we decided to keep the cordon in place until we were sure that we had searched every house for him.

I was right – he was still in the flats. I received a communiqué from DCS Orr back at headquarters telling me that Graham had phoned a newspaper reporter and told him that he had new hostages – an elderly couple named Robb, whose flat he had forced his way into. He had been trying to flee but was beaten by the speed of the police cordon, so he had taken the hostage route again. The couple's flat had been visited by officers during the evacuation process but when there was no reply they had assumed the house was empty.

Graham was trying to use the press to pressurise the police and had stated that he would only give himself up to the reporter, who had been given permission by headquarters to go to the door of the flat to talk to Graham. I told them in no uncertain terms that this would not happen and made my feelings abundantly clear before switching off my radio link in disgust. I would not allow this hare-brained scheme to go forward and give Graham the opportunity to take yet another civilian hostage.

We had achieved a phone link-up with the house and were using the janitor's room as a base for operations. Harry Bell was a trained negotiator and he took on the job of talking to Graham. The first thing was to make him realise that he was going nowhere and that he was not in control of the situation. Harry struck up a reasonable rapport on the phone, to such an extent that at one point he asked Graham to come out onto the balcony of the flat and speak to us face-to-face.

Apparently, the reporter had told DCS Orr that Graham did not trust me. I had never dealt with Graham, so I do not know how he had come to this conclusion. I suspected it to be a ploy on the hack's part to get himself into the centre of the story. Maybe he realised he could not manipulate me as easily as the officers at headquarters. Nevertheless, despite my presence, Graham came out onto the balcony. He showed no sign of recognition but it was not the time to pursue that little mystery. I let Harry do the talking.

'What weapons have you got, Danny?' he asked.

'A knife,' said Graham. We could see it in his hand.

'Surely you don't intend to hurt these old folk,' said Harry, 'so it would be better if you throw us your knife down.'

Amazingly, Graham complied. We now had the weapon but we weren't naive enough not to take into account the possibility that he might have had other weapons within the house. It was, however, a great psychological boost to us that Graham was bending to our will and starting to cooperate.

We returned to the janitor's office, where Harry again spoke on the phone to Graham. It was late afternoon. Harry asked for the release of the old lady but Graham again said he wanted to speak to the reporter. The man was still on site and I had him brought to the janitor's office, where I allowed him to speak to Graham for all of two minutes before he was ushered out again.

Harry then managed to talk Graham into releasing Mrs Robb. The second-floor landing had been completely secured by the Firearms Unit. I joined them in order to check for myself the situation with the old lady. A controlled exit was achieved. Armed officers escorted her out of the building carrying her handbag and purse, which she said she did not want to leave in the house with 'that horrible young man'.

We were getting there. Harry was well in control of the telephone conversation with Graham and continued to press for the release of Mr Robb. Throughout his negotiations with Harry, Graham had been watching television and listening to radio reports and there is no doubt that he was now the person to be terrified that should he make a wrong move it might be a fatal one. He was having a taste of what it felt like to be trapped. He said that he would release his final hostage if we could guarantee his safety. It was amazing how quickly this desperate criminal, who had terrorised two families, had turned into a snivelling coward frightened for his own skin.

Slightly before 6 p.m., Graham said that he was ready to release Mr Robb but there was a problem. The old man would not leave without his pension book. Mrs Robb was afraid her headstrong husband was liable to become angry and fight with Graham. Harry and I couldn't believe that after this crazy 24 hours a bloody pension book was causing a major drama in the release of the final hostage.

Eventually, the pension book was found and old Mr Robb was released, again into the hands of the Firearms Unit, and reunited with his wife just in time for the six o'clock news.

A strange thing then took place. Harry was still in contact with

Graham by phone. He turned to me and said that Graham told him he would come out when he saw the news broadcasts. I looked at Harry and said, 'Remind him that he's in that house on his own now. Tell him that if he doesn't get his arse to the front door right now, I'm coming right in there after him.'

This got the required response from Graham and he came to the front door with his hands in the air. The Firearms Unit moved in, guns levelled, threw him to the ground and searched him carefully.

I was still quite intrigued about the claim that Graham didn't trust me. I decided to accompany him in the car from the flats to Govan Police Office.

'So,' I said, 'I hear you don't like that cop Joe Jackson.'

'Never met the guy,' said Graham, confirming what I already suspected. 'Never had any dealings with him.'

That particular scribbler and I never really saw eye to eye after this incident.

The police had achieved a great deal on this day. For us it had started with the news of the family being taken hostage and the demand for £150,000 to be stolen from the security company. Ten and a half hours later it was all over. The family had been found reasonably safe and well, a further two hostages had been released safely and three desperate criminals were under lock and key. We had also recovered a shotgun, a handgun, knives and an open razor, and no money had changed hands. When the case went to court, the judge castigated the three men, labelling them as terrorists because of their actions in entering a family's home, wearing masks and brandishing a variety of weapons. Daniel Graham was sentenced to a total of 18 years. Raymond Graham was sentenced to 15 years, and Sean Garty to 12 years in prison.

After the case had been dealt with, a daily newspaper ran a picture of the Robbs with the reporter, describing how, thanks to his heroic actions, he was responsible for their release. They chose not to mention the hard work by the many police officers that day or, in particular,

John Burke, who had taken part in a very fraught and difficult police operation to free his entire family. If anyone was a hero that day, it was certainly him.

BABY SNATCH

The thing about being a police officer is that you should never really be off duty. If you are out for a night – as my brother and I were when we saw Big Arthur force that van off the road – and you spot a crime, then a good cop must become involved. This is doubly true if you are a senior officer.

Although I was in charge of the CID in the busiest division in Strathclyde crime-wise, I still had to take my turns at weekends covering the full region. There was always a senior detective on call and I knew that, even if I was at home, the chances were that I would be summoned. One Saturday night, the phone rang at about 8 p.m. On the other end of the phone was the inspector in charge of the Control Room at force headquarters.

'There's been a wee kiddie snatched in Dumbarton,' he told me. 'Taken from her pram while she was sleeping in her grandmother's garden. We can't get in touch with the local boss out there, so it looks like you're up.'

'Does the divisional commander know?'

'Aye – there have been searches ongoing but he wants a senior CID presence.'

I left my home on Glasgow's south side and broke speed limits to reach Dumbarton, to the north-east of the city. At the local headquarters, I found out a bit more about the incident. The four-month-old baby girl was the only child of a nice young couple who had left her that afternoon in the care of her grandmother, who had taken the child in her pram into the centre of the town, returning home between 5 and 6 p.m. The baby was asleep by that time and, not wishing to disturb her, her grandmother left the pram in her garden near to the back door so that she would hear her if she cried. But it only takes a second for someone to make off with a child. The grandmother got the shock of her life when she went out and found the pram empty.

She alerted the police and everything was done by the book. In such situations, you have to act quickly and hit the ground running. You can't afford to sit and have a cup of coffee while you contemplate your navel. You have a missing child and that conjures up various scenarios, none of which bear thinking about. Detectives interviewed the mother, father and grandmother at the station. Uniformed officers combed the surrounding area, hunting through houses, garages, outhouses and sheds. An alert was circulated to all offices throughout Strathclyde and beyond. The officers involved knew their job and they did it well.

My first thoughts were of who to use in such a situation. The press was one of my strategies; I realised it would be necessary to involve the public in order to have the best chance of a speedy recovery of the child unharmed. It can be a bit of a long shot but in this type of situation you take any shot you can, as quickly as you can. I contacted the Control Room and asked the inspector in charge to call up the various news agencies and TV stations in order to get as much coverage as possible. This worked like a charm and the broadcasts on radio and television went out throughout Scotland. The media generally could not have been more helpful.

Time was wearing on and the situation was becoming more fraught. There had not been any sightings of the child and her family were totally distraught. They had remained at the police station and were given as much comfort as possible but all they wanted, all they prayed for, was the return of the child. The grandmother in particular was inconsolable, blaming herself when there was no need – many parents and grandparents daily leave their child in the confines of their gardens to sleep in the fresh air.

About 1 a.m., with no sightings of the child and searches being extended, a young detective phoned me from Oban, 80 miles north-west of Dumbarton. A local family had seen the TV news report about the missing child and told him that they had earlier seen a local woman, a rather strange character who lived alone, carrying a baby into her house. The family had put two and two together and thankfully made four. Two local detectives spoke to them and then called on the woman in question. They asked to see the child. It was indeed the missing baby. The local casualty surgeon examined her and pronounced that she had not been harmed. A journey to Oban from Dumbarton, by predominantly winding country roads, normally takes in excess of two hours, so I tried to arrange for the police helicopter to uplift the child. It was unavailable, so the baby, in the care of a young policewoman, was delivered to Dumbarton in a fast car. The family was naturally more than delighted to have her back safe and sound and a photograph of the baby being handed back to them made front-page news on the Sunday morning.

Her abductor was arrested and found not only to be suffering from severe depression but also a pre-existing mental condition. I believe she was treated leniently when she appeared at court and subsequently received the medical treatment she so obviously required.

I wish everything in police work would go as smoothly as it did that particular evening. Undoubtedly, the work of the officers attending the initial missing child call, the prompt action of the Oban detectives and the help of the media together laid the foundations for a quick resolution to this incident. It shows what can be achieved in a relatively short space of time.

This contrasts totally with the policing fiasco surrounding the much-publicised abduction in Portugal in 2007 of three-year-old Madeleine McCann. When it was discovered that Madeleine had been taken from her bed, the local police were contacted. However, proper searches and interviews did not take place immediately. Whether this was due to a lack of experience on the part of the Portuguese police or a lack of understanding of the seriousness of the situation does not matter. What it led to was a total media circus, speculation and, at the time of writing, no resolution – little Madeleine is still missing.

Swift and correct solutions are always the answer. Unfortunately, there is a developing trend in Britain to go into long, drawn-out investigations fuelled by incorrect methods and lack of experience. When this occurs, not only in connection with abductions but also other high-profile crimes or incidents, it invariably leads to a media frenzy provoking all types of weird and wonderful theories. For proof of this, one has to look no further than the disappearance of Madeleine McCann or, for that matter, the Princess Diana crash inquiry.

AN UNNECESSARY DEATH

Police officers can get very frustrated when dealing with the Procurator Fiscal's Office. The Fiscal is the Scottish equivalent of the Crown Prosecution Authority in England or, I suppose, the American District Attorney. It is the Fiscal who decides if a case will proceed to court and will then guide it through the system. In short, the police make the arrests, the Fiscal puts them away. That's the theory, anyway. Most senior fiscals are officials with great experience and respect for the senior police officers they deal with. This, however, does not mean that the two sides always see eye to eye and this can cause a certain amount of friction in the relationship.

One of the problems that can arise, in the opinion of many police officers, is that there can be too much of a buddy-buddy relationship between lawyers representing the accused and those of the Fiscal's Office. Police officers and their involvement in certain cases can be seen as a bit of a nuisance when deals are being done between the supposedly opposing sides. As far as I'm concerned, these deals arouse the ire of the victims and their families, and are generally to the detriment of the public interest.

This certainly applied in the murder of Beryl Woyka, an 80-year-old widow staying on her own in a luxury apartment block in wealthy

Pollokshields on the south side of Glasgow. I firmly believe that her violent death could have been avoided.

At the time, Govan was suffering a spate of robberies of elderly pensioners who were being mugged as they left the local post offices after collecting their meagre pensions. The main targets were usually old women whose handbags were snatched. The attackers were three young men, who were not above punching and kicking the old people in order to relieve them of their cash. The problem was, the descriptions given could have matched the majority of youths roaming the streets of Govan. Steps were taken to ensure that police officers were in the vicinity of the post offices on pension day, while other inquiries continued in an effort to trace the young neds responsible. It wasn't until the gang made a mistake that there was a breakthrough in the case.

Two male pensioners who lived together in a ground-floor flat off Paisley Road West had gone to collect their pensions then returned home. They had no sooner entered their house than they heard the sound of someone lifting the flap of their letter box and the noise of people outside their door. One of the old men went to the door and as he opened it three youths burst in. The first man was knocked to the floor, where he was punched and kicked before the trio rampaged into the flat and subjected the other old man to the same brutal treatment. The gang then made off with the men's pensions.

We were informed about this latest attack and quickly linked it to those committed outside the post offices. Obviously, the increased police presence had forced the neds to resort to home invasion in order to line their pockets. The two elderly victims were considerably shaken by their ordeal and, as would be expected, their descriptions of the three criminals were not terribly good. This time, though, we had a crime scene to be forensically examined. Our scene-of-crime experts from headquarters were sent for and the house was given a thorough inspection. And we got lucky. During the examination of the letter box, a fingerprint impression was found on the inside of the flap. A fingerprint is only of use if you have a match and here we were lucky again – it was on record. The print related to a young Govan criminal who had convictions for violence and drug abuse.

The young man was brought in for interview. He burst like a balloon. He confessed his involvement and gave up his pals – one being his brother, the other a long-time associate. Both had similar backgrounds, histories of violence and a record of drug abuse. They needed the cash to fuel their habit and, like most users, they did not care who they hurt to get it. The sad thing is they were aged between 15 and 17 and were already raging heroin addicts. Even so, they were despicable wee tykes. When all three were interviewed, they admitted all the muggings at the post offices plus the attacks on the old men at their home.

They were charged with five counts of assault and robbery and a case was prepared for the Procurator Fiscal. In doing so, I ensured that a paragraph was inserted giving the full reasons as to why they should not be considered for bail. When an accused person is charged with serious crimes, it is within the power of the Procurator Fiscal to request the court to hold them in custody until the date of their trial. This would not have been amiss in the case of these three young skulls for their previous misdeeds and was, as far as I am concerned, an absolute necessity. I firmly believed that if released they would commit further acts of violence in order to feed their drug addiction. It was in their nature and, thanks to the smack, in their blood.

It was a very comprehensive police report but for reasons unknown to me the plea was disregarded – the three were released on bail later that day.

Three days later, the body of an old woman was discovered in her home by a home help. She was lying on her bed, fully clothed, but had obviously received a savage beating. Her name was Beryl Woyka. I had just come on duty when I was told about the discovery and

I went to the plush flat with a squad of officers. We arrived just as the forensics team pulled up, so we entered the flat together. The scene of the crime was pretty horrific. The walls of the living room were spattered with blood and there was a trail through the hallway and into the bedroom, which told us that the poor woman had been dragged through before being thrown onto the bed. The house had been ransacked. Drawers had been tipped out, wardrobes emptied, cupboards plundered.

My squad immediately began door-to-door inquiries but found that most of the neighbours were out at work. There was a controlled entry to the block of six flats but of a type that can be easily overcome and no cameras monitored the entrance. Old Mrs Woyka therefore was probably the only occupant present for most of the day, unfortunately making her an easy target.

Once the body had been examined at the crime locus by the casualty surgeon and removed to the police mortuary, the forensic team got to work. They examined the entire flat minutely and recovered a plethora of fingerprints, which were lifted and sent to headquarters for examination and comparison. I was not surprised in the slightest by the results.

The fingerprints of the three hoodlums so recently released from custody were all over Mrs Woyka's house. We rounded them up again and charged them, this time with murder. This time they were remanded in custody and the various assaults and robberies plus the murder would be dealt with together at the High Court. It was too late, though, for their victim, who had died a horrific death. As usual in a case of murder, there was a post-mortem examination to establish the cause of death. Two or more pathologists conduct these in the presence of senior detective officers and a member of the Procurator Fiscal's department. Mrs Woyka had several fractures to her skull, about five broken ribs and various internal injuries as well as external cuts and bruises. Her heart had also apparently failed during this horrible attack. It did not strike me until later that the Fiscal present seemed to labour the fact with the pathologists that Mrs Woyka had died from a heart attack.

In such cases, statements are submitted by all relevant witnesses and, being the senior investigating officer, I submitted mine to the Fiscal's Department as I had done on every occasion when I was in charge of a case. I duly awaited the arrival of my citation for court. I was very surprised when all other officers involved received theirs but there was none for me. Neither was I precognosed, which are interviews carried out by the Fiscal's Department and the lawyer of the accused during which they go over your statement prior to the trial.

I began to smell a rat. The procedures seemed wrong to me and I asked my own officers what had taken place at their precognitions. All became clear when I learned that the Fiscal's Department and the Crown had decided to drop the initial charges, that of the home invasion, against these three criminals. There was a lack of evidence, they said – despite the admissions of the accused and the fingerprints found on the old men's letter box. To add insult to injury, it appeared that Mrs Woyka's death was now to be prosecuted as a culpable homicide rather than murder, which ultimately would carry a much lesser sentence. By dropping the other charges, the Crown could simply proceed on the death of Mrs Woyka without revealing the complete cock-up they had made by allowing these three criminals out on bail. By reducing the charges, it meant they were accepting that she had died of a heart attack instead of the terror and the savage beating which had caused that heart attack. The penny dropped for me regarding the actions and thoughts of the Fiscal at the post-mortem and I felt that they had already been in the process of looking for an escape route for letting these neds loose on the streets. I was not to be cited because they did not want me spilling the beans on the stand.

I, along with other officers, was furious at this turn of events and decided to take my own course of action. I contacted some acquaintances – who just happened to be newspaper reporters – and told them what I suspected was happening. I was so incensed at what was going on that I was prepared to resign from the police and reveal the extent to which justice was being ignored in order to save some bureaucrat's skin. My proposed actions somehow reached the ears of the Crown, which was not a surprise.

Although not called to give evidence at the High Court, I turned up anyway and sat in an obvious position in the gallery. The reporters I had contacted were in the court waiting for the neds to appear and the fireworks I had quietly promised. As I had not been cited, I was able to sit in the front row of the public benches. I made myself obvious to the court officials and lawyers, who were quite aware of my displeasure. The prosecutor was the Solicitor General; I knew him from previous trials. Before the court got under way, he signalled to me to join him in a small office off the main courtroom. He told me that the neds were liable to plead guilty, then went on to try to explain to me why the prosecution was not proceeding with other charges against the accused, citing the fact that the elderly witnesses could not properly identify the accused. I reminded him of their admissions and the fingerprint evidence from the old men's house. We then discussed the likelihood of a ridiculously lenient sentence for the accused, when and if they pled guilty, as the judge, Lord King Murray, had in my opinion handed out liberal sentences in the past. The Solicitor General assured me that this would not occur, as the senior Scottish judge had come through from Edinburgh and was waiting within the judge's chambers to consult with and advise Lord King Murray on the proper sentencing of these three dangerous youths. Somewhat reassured regarding the sentencing but still seething about the other charges being dropped, I resumed my seat in the main courtroom.

The waiting reporters and I were on the edges of our seats as the three accused were brought into court to face Lord King Murray. As expected, they all pleaded guilty to the charge of culpable homicide. Normally, a list of the previous convictions of the accused would be produced and the accused could well be remanded in custody for later sentencing once background reports by criminal justice workers were made available. These reports would then be scrutinised followed by sentencing. This did not happen on this occasion. The learned judge, after hearing the guilty pleas, left the bench and returned to his chambers, where he remained for five minutes or so before returning. He then proceeded to sentence the eldest of the trio to 12 years' imprisonment, the other two each receiving 10 years – reasonable sentences, in my opinion, and more than I expected, although not enough for these vicious young hoodlums.

Would I really have gone through with my threat to resign? Maybe, maybe not, but as some measure of justice had been achieved, I wasn't put in the position of having to decide.

The Kilmarnock Moors Murder

I had been a detective superintendent for five years and was completely at ease in the role. In fact, I had reached the stage in my professional development where I relished the thought of a hard nut to crack. One Saturday morning in early June 1989, when I was still in charge of Govan CID and also the on-call senior detective in charge of criminal investigation for all of Strathclyde, I was sitting at a desk in police headquarters at Pitt Street, settling down to a cup of coffee and a bacon roll. I had no idea that one of the trickiest and most rewarding cases of my career was about to come my way.

It began with the appearance at my office door of a Drug Squad detective sergeant, Stevie Heath, looking slightly flustered and wanting advice. His team had just lifted a man and his wife from Millerston on a charge of dealing drugs. Although there was nothing unusual about that, the tale they told was quite out of the ordinary. The couple were talking about a drug-related murder that had taken place some months earlier.

Stevie was looking not just for direction but also for someone to take charge and I was happy to oblige, this being right up my street. This case was to become very much my baby. I should say at this juncture that putting effort into locating and locking up all serious criminals was not the philosophy of all senior officers. Some would have shied away under such a challenge. I was perhaps too stupid to take the easy route and would not walk away. I could easily have passed this to a division and washed my hands of it. You can call it what you want – professionalism, low boredom threshold, arrogance – but it was not my style.

A senior investigating officer is only as good as the team working with him and due to the nature of this case I decided to get a squad together comprising officers from both the Drug Squad and Serious Crime Squad. Their first remit was to round up and detain the local criminals who had been named by the husband and wife as having taken part in the murder. In a very short time, three men – small-time crooks Thomas Collins, Thomas Currie and Stephen Mitchell – were hoovered up and duly made tape-recorded voluntary statements. They each admitted having been involved in the murder of a drugs courier and burying his body somewhere on the Fenwick Moors, a vast stretch of rough, largely open countryside between Kilmarnock and Glasgow. They also named two other men as having been involved: Glasgow man John Paul McFadyen and a Spaniard called Ricardo Blanco. Neither was the type you would invite to Sunday dinner. McFadyen was a real tough customer and the only one out of the gang who did not burst under questioning. Blanco, a French-born Spaniard who claimed to have killed a man while deserting from the Foreign Legion, was known either as 'The Mad Spaniard' or 'Ricardo the Hit-man'. He and McFadyen had supposedly hacked at the buttocks and anus of a German drug courier in Spain in order to get at the drugs he carried in condoms in his stomach. Because of McFadyen's refusal to talk, I had more contact with Blanco, whom I found to be a boastful, vain character who thought he was smarter than everyone around him.

So far, we had no idea of the identity of the victim, knowing only that his name was Paul. We knew the murder involved amphetamines being brought into Scotland from St Paul's, a multicultural and very socially challenged part of Bristol, where the drug trade was controlled by Rastafarians. The Rasta boss was Lennox Gayle and it was he who had sent the courier to Glasgow with £30,000 worth of amphetamine sulphate, or speed, as well as temazepam and temgesic, to be sold to a mob of would-be hard men, led by McFadyen. McFadyen was at the time resident in England, while Blanco had a base in Bristol. They had set up the deal with Lennox Gayle and then recruited the three Glasgow neds to assist them, with a view to ripping off the supplier. McFadyen's father was also involved in drug trafficking and the resultant court case but took no part in the murder.

One Saturday in October 1988, the courier arrived in Glasgow Central Station with a female known only as 'Scouse' in tow, carrying the drugs in a holdall. The gang met them off the train and took them first to a flat in Parkhead, where they proceeded to smoke a relaxing batch of cannabis. They were then to head off to a country cottage in Ayrshire, to the south-west of Glasgow, where they would be safe until the drugs had been punted and Paul could return to Bristol with the cash due to his boss. The courier was out of his head and thought nothing of the strange plan. Scouse, however, smelled rodent through the pungent aroma of weed. She was not happy with the set-up and decided she wanted to go back to Bristol that evening. Later, when I eventually managed to speak to her, she told me that she had felt something was very wrong with the situation and had actually heard McFadyen and Blanco discussing what they should do with the couriers, so she decided she was for the off. She managed to persuade one of the Glasgow neds, Currie, to give her a run back to the station, which undoubtedly saved her life.

The gang and the courier set off for this presumably mythical cottage in the country in a van they had hired for the job. They made one significant stop on the way – to buy a spade. They told the courier this was to be used to bury the merchandise and the young man, high on cannabis, took their words at face value. They also stopped for fish and chips. Later, the gang joked about this being Paul's 'Last Supper'.

They then headed towards the A77 through the south side of the city and eventually cut into smaller side roads until, as far as I could make out from their later descriptions of the area, they reached a small village called Moscow, to the north-east of Kilmarnock. The villains then took the unsuspecting courier into a wooded area. Blanco was walking behind the doomed young man, carrying a concealed sawn-off shotgun. At some point, he pulled out the gun and pulled the trigger. The shotgun blast apparently blew off the young man's jaw but did not kill him, so other members of the gang then took turns at firing into his body as he lay on the ground.

Then the real purpose of the spade was revealed. They dug a grave and tipped the bullet-riddled corpse into it. However, they may have been efficient as cold-blooded killers but they were not as adept as gravediggers. The hole was too shallow and one of their victim's feet remained in view. Too lazy to dig a deeper hole, they found an old mattress lying nearby and threw it over the protruding foot. The gang then returned to Glasgow, where they decided to finish a good night's work by picking up prostitutes.

My team's priority was to find the body, so the three suspects were taken to the moors between Moscow and Galston, where they tried to pinpoint the makeshift grave. At its height, the hunt was conducted by about a hundred uniformed officers, led by Support Unit officers who were specially trained for such searches. Although we concentrated on the area indicated by the accused, they had been very vague. City boys, they were unused to the topography of the countryside. Add the passage of time to the fact that they had been smoking cannabis along with their victim and you realise why their memory was flawed. The search area covered 30 or so square miles of harsh woodland and moor. I went up in a helicopter rented by the police to survey the territory concerned and to be quite honest I was shocked at the sheer size and scale of what we were attempting, considering that the body had been lying for at least eight or nine months. We used heat-seeking cameras to try and pinpoint the shallow grave and borrowed dogs from West Yorkshire that were specially trained to find buried bodies. Although the search team was slightly scaled down during the investigation, the hunt was still running at the time of the trial.

A number of other things were happening and my team at Kilmarnock was following up other leads. From their statements, we already knew that the gang had bought a spade to bury the body. After the murder, they had gone to Royston in Glasgow where they had burnt the courier's belongings and ditched the spade. When I read the statement, I knew that Glasgow bin men would not throw out a new spade. Detective Inspector Eric Pile went to the depot to trace the team responsible for the area at the operative time, ten months previously. Within two days, he had tracked them all down and pinpointed the man who had found the spade, who had taken it home; it was in his garden shed. We had it forensically examined but found nothing of use. The spade had been bought in a shop at Glasgow Cross. Eric managed to get the till receipt showing the sale of the spade. This was very helpful because it was dated and timed, and backed up the statements already given by the gang.

It was also claimed that the shotgun had been thrown into the Clyde to join the hundreds of other weapons littering the bottom of the river. All we knew was that it had been thrown off a bridge, so the river was dragged near every bridge spanning the water. We did not find the weapon.

One of the things you do not do as an SIO is reveal everything to the press at the beginning of an inquiry. It never ceases to amaze me: the present trend by police forces, particularly those in foreign countries, to disclose as much as they can at the outset. In this case, I did not announce until well into the inquiry that the murder victim had been buried in a shallow grave and covered by a mattress that had been found nearby. When I did decide to reveal this to journalists, it was in the hope that it would help the investigation to ask the public to identify illegal dumping grounds in the area and report any old mattresses that had been left lying about. Within a week of making this plea, we had reports of 168 mattresses on the moor. None of them concealed any grisly secrets.

The body was never found. Whether we were looking in the wrong place, whether we had been steered in the wrong direction by the suspects, or whether someone had returned after the murder and removed the corpse, I cannot say. A murder inquiry without a body is rare. A corpse can yield all manner of evidence – not least, proof that a murder has, in fact, taken place – and to make a case without one is difficult, but not impossible.

During the first week of the inquiry, various pieces of information came at the team from all directions and one of my jobs was to ensure that I had enough evidence to convince the Procurator Fiscal that the suspects should be held in custody. Sometimes, this is not an easy thing to do, as fiscals would often prefer to take the easier option and release the neds on bail. Three of the gang were initially locked up on the strength of their confessions plus the information from the touts. McFadyen, it turned out, was already in jail waiting to stand trial for a separate gun offence. His dad was in on drugs charges. Ricardo Blanco was, as I later learned, in Spain. This was shaping up to be rather a tricky and difficult case to pull together.

On top of this, I did not have the complete backing of the hierarchy at headquarters at Pitt Street. Many desk-bound officers, especially those at headquarters, were perplexed by this inquiry and could not understand my methods or indeed why I even wished to continue with it. If any of them had been faced with the challenge, I'm sure the initial information would have been written off as nonsense and no further action or investigation would have taken place. The Chief Constable at this time was an Englishman named Sloan. He and I had met before and we didn't like each other. At our first meeting, while I was still in charge of the Serious Crime Squad, he asked if I had any supergrasses. I replied in the negative, saying I did not agree with this English idea and believed that anyone involved in that level of criminality should be in jail themselves. I don't think he appreciated my comments.

We faced very tight time constraints, and I was more or less running three Major Incident Rooms. The main one was in Kilmarnock: officers there dealt with the search for the body as well as compiling the various pieces of the complex jigsaw that eventually became the basis of the Crown's case. The second Incident Room was at Clydebank and dealt with drug-dealing transactions that had occurred before the murder but from which I was able to tie the gang together within the west of Scotland. Last, but by no means least, there was a linked Incident Room in Bristol, where the dead courier had come from; manned by very able and helpful officers from the local CID, its task was to deal with any information we gathered that would help in identifying the victim.

The case, though, was not looking so hot. We had five suspects under lock and key, including the McFadyens, father and son, but we didn't know where the body was or even the victim's full name. We didn't have a weapon or any of the drugs supposedly carried north. We didn't know the real name of the girl who had been with the courier and who had so narrowly missed becoming a victim herself.

My watchword to my teams on this inquiry was to ask for 'a wee winner' each day. By this I meant that with their continued hard work and support, small but extremely important pieces of the puzzle could be put in place. As a result of this approach, we steadily built an excellent case. While my own teams in Scotland were producing the goods, the Bristol cops came up with a real gem. They learned that Ricardo Blanco was due to fly into Bristol from Spain. The problem was, at this point, I did not have a murder warrant for him. The Procurator Fiscal at Kilmarnock refused to back the issue of such a warrant, as he maintained I had investigative proof of a murder but no evidence linking Blanco to it. There are, however, ways and means. I pulled a wee stroke and decided to go in a different direction: I approached another Procurator Fiscal, this time in Dumbarton, which covered the Clydebank area where I had my second Incident Room. I decided to ask him for a warrant for the Spaniard's arrest. I called into play two of the Drug Squad, who were already part of my team, and I told them not to go home that night until they had unearthed a good solid case for a drugs supply warrant for Ricardo Blanco. Time was running short, as he was due to arrive in Britain the following day. The two officers, a male and a female detective constable, delved through every piece of information we had on the gang members and every applicable piece of drugs legislation. Very early the following morning, I met with them at Clydebank and they presented me with an extremely prima facie case. I invited them to attend the Fiscal's Office at Dumbarton with me that morning to present their evidence. They, of course, would also be available to discuss any of the intricacies involving the drugs.

The Procurator Fiscal pored over the paperwork and asked several questions regarding the information contained within it. I was unable to answer the drugs questions but my experts could. He was satisfied and with a great flourish signed the papers to grant an apprehension warrant. The following evening, local officers accompanied by four of my men met a very surprised Blanco as he walked off the plane at Bristol. He was bundled into a car and driven overnight by my burly Glasgow detectives to Scotland.

My first meeting with Blanco was in an interview room in Clydebank Police Office where he was questioned under caution. From the outset, he admitted his part in the killing, saying that he was the first to shoot the courier and that his shot took away the courier's jaw. Blanco was a boastful character and really thought that he had impressed me with his bravado. He told me how they had buried the courier, and he relished the telling, little realising that he was also digging his own grave. I interviewed him twice more and it was he who eventually identified the courier as being Paul Leslie

Thorne, a young man involved, to a small extent, in the drugs scene in Bristol. Blanco was crazy enough to think that by giving me this help, I would help him to escape justice. More fool him. He really believed that he was calling the shots. My team and I realised – and not for the first time – that it is amazing what maturity and a smile can achieve when dealing with fools.

So now we had a name for the victim. What we needed was to identify the young woman who had come up to Glasgow with him from Bristol and who had sensed something wrong with the set-up. We knew her simply as 'Scouse', so it was a fair surmise that she hailed from Liverpool. Armed with this information, the Bristol detectives managed to trace her. It turned out that she was the girlfriend of, and was totally controlled by, Lennox Gayle, the Rastafarian Mr Big. She refused to speak to the Bristol officers about the events or even admit to ever being in Glasgow. She was, however, found in possession of a false passport, for which she was arrested, and this was enough to hold her in custody for the time being.

I needed to speak to this witness on my own ground – and in order to do that I needed to get to Gayle. We had learned that a Rastafarian crony of Gayle's had been punting drugs in Clydebank during the year before the murder. I therefore requested another drugs warrant, this time for Gayle and his mate. That was phase one; phase two was getting the pair of them out of Bristol. They were hard gangsters and the cops down there had to go in heavy-handed to take them into custody. I had a team of my own men there, all big guys, waiting to escort the two dealers back to Scotland once they had been dragged from their dens. They were brought up in separate vehicles through the night and by the time they were in an interview room in Glasgow they were tired and slightly disorientated by the course and speed of events. I'm sure they fully expected the big, bad men of Glasgow CID to tear their heads off.

I was looking forward to talking to Gayle, as I was sure that if treated properly he could be one of the keys to the whole case. I had the two men brought to Clydebank Police Office, where they arrived in the early hours of a Saturday morning, which gave me the whole weekend with them in custody; I had planned when they would be arrested so that I could have as much time as possible with them.

I had researched the habits of the Rastafarian cult. They habitually smoked dope and took other drugs but supposedly never touched meat or alcohol, which to me is a very strange way of life. By the time they arrived in Scotland, the suspects were well strung out and would have known that a heavy jail sentence for drug dealing possibly lay ahead of them. As prisoners in custody, they were given breakfast, in this case two bread rolls with flat sausage. At lunchtime, they were given two mutton pies. Funnily enough, they did not eat their meals. This was not a strategy to break them down – it was just that the turnkey, who had the job of looking after the prisoners, was perhaps not aware of their specific eating habits.

I was not available until late afternoon to start the interviews. It was a very warm summer's day and the cells are not the best place to be in such conditions. So when I felt the time was right, I had Gayle brought to my room. This was a strategy to make Gayle amenable to my questioning. His dreadlocks looked as if they could have housed a family of bats and he did not seem very pleased to see me. I started, as always, by asking if he had any complaints about his treatment while in our custody. This apparently took him by surprise: he was ready for a heavy session of questioning rather than enquiries after his well-being. Caught on the hop, he started to tell me that he had not been fed properly, having been given only meaty things, which did not suit his vegetarian tastes. Although this had been a genuine oversight, I capitalised on it by calling in one of my detectives and feigning disgust that Gayle and his friend had not received proper Scottish hospitality. I then asked Gayle if he liked Indian food, making a great play of taking money from my own pocket and sending out for a meal, including vegetable pakora. I knew that English folk generally had not tasted pakora, or the spicy sauce supplied with it.

When the meal arrived, in order to show that I was not trying to poison him, I had some pakora as well. It proved to be a hit with him and he tucked in with great gusto. Then the nippy sauce began to kick in. I had asked my detective to make sure it was extra hot, the way I liked it. Gayle showed signs of relaxing during our meal and began to talk. I asked him if he would like something to drink with his eats. He agreed that this would be very nice. I just happened to have two bottles in my desk, one of lemonade and one of whisky. I felt I had to show him proper Scottish hospitality. Despite his Rastafarian strictures, he agreed to share a dram. I poured him a generous measure. My prime objective in this move was to convince Gayle that I was a good guy and not someone who was against all criminals. Of course, nothing could have been further from the truth. The game plan was to win his confidence. This unexpected treatment had helped make him pretty relaxed and even jolly. I brought up the topic of his girlfriend, Scouse, who was still locked up in Bristol. Scouse was a totally crucial witness due to her involvement with the murder victim and his killers. I suggested to Gayle that he should persuade her to come to Scotland to assist us. Amazingly, I had managed to have her standing by a phone in prison, in order that Gayle could tell her to 'get her arse up to Scotland to help the nice police officers'. He was extremely helpful, although we had been told by Bristol CID that he was the worst villain that they had and would never assist the police. The phrase 'there is more than one way to skin a cat' comes to mind. Perhaps the Bristol lads had not tried being nice to their local crooks and showing them some sympathy and understanding. Sometimes, being smart is better than being hard.

Also, it has to be remembered, the accused had not only murdered one of Gayle's people, they had tried to rip him off. These were not actions designed to endear them to him, although no doubt he would have much preferred to have dealt with the matter in his own way than involve the law.

After Lennox had a quick chat with Scouse on the phone, I spoke to her. She said that now that she had his permission, she was prepared to help and readily agreed to come north. In the hope that my strategy would succeed, I had already organised a release order and had a car standing by at the prison where she was being held. When the case came to trial, she turned up looking like a schoolmarm and provided telling evidence, identifying all of the accused that had been with her and Paul Thorne at the flat shortly before he was taken to the Fenwick Moors and killed. Gayle was also extremely forthcoming and was used as a witness regarding his testimony about meeting the gang to set up the drugs buy and sending Thorne and Scouse as the couriers.

Nevertheless, as a way of underlining the possibility that he could be charged for drug offences, I had Gayle put in an identification parade to be viewed by other witnesses. Naturally, being black, we filled the line-up with other black men. However, his distinctive Rasta hairstyle would have set him apart from other men in the line-up. We got round this by having every man in the parade wear a rolled-up plastic shopping bag on his head. That identification parade was perhaps one of the most unusual I've ever witnessed.

Lennox Gayle, Scouse and Gayle's pal were all in Glasgow for two weeks during the trial. I had them staying in the Police Training School at Oxford Street to ensure they did not go missing or get up to no good. It cost me every night for a load of pakora and curries. Gayle apparently put aside his abstinence from alcohol and had developed a taste for whisky and brandy, as was evident by the empty bottles each night in their bins.

The High Court proceedings for this case began in October 1989 in the Sheriff Court Building in Glasgow's Carlton Place, a sprawling, modern construction on the south side of the river. Lasting 47 days, it became the longest-running murder trial in the history of the Scottish courts, although it was overtaken a few years later when Paul Ferris was accused and cleared of gunning down young Arthur Thompson. There were six men in the dock. John Ross McFadyen had been charged with drug offences. His son, John Paul McFadyen, along with Ricardo Blanco, Thomas Collins, Thomas Currie and Stephen Mitchell were all charged with the murder of Paul Leslie Thorne as well as with drug and firearms offences.

At the start of the trial, there was unprecedented security within the Sheriff Court. Everybody, including QCs and lawyers, was searched before entering the court, as there seemed to be an amazing number of neds hanging about in the corridors. I noticed this as I turned up for the first day of the trial and I spoke to the court officers to make sure that everyone in and around the building was checked out. This case was very high profile, involving many witnesses who would not normally give evidence for the prosecution in a trial; the fear was that they would be intimidated by friends of the accused. As it turned out, it was another form of intimidation that was brought to my attention. On the third day of the trial, I was in the court building, although not in the court itself as I had not yet given evidence, keeping an eye on what was happening, when I was approached by a Procurator Fiscal involved in the case. He asked me if I would like to take a walk outside with him. As we strolled along the banks of the River Clyde, he said he had a rather delicate request to make. I wondered what was coming, then he told me that the QCs and lawyers representing the accused were unnerved and intimidated by my presence in the building. I really could not understand this, as I am a rather mild-mannered chap. I was only making sure that there were no underhand methods taking place around the court. He then asked me not to turn up again until the date of my citation. I blithely ignored his request. It was never repeated.

The presiding judge for the case was Lord Allanbridge and Kevin Drummond QC presented the case for the Crown. He was up against a veritable posse of the top lawyers in Scotland. Each of the accused had at least two lawyers defending on their team, including Donald Findlay, Edgar Prais, Bill Taylor, Bill Dunlop and other very notable QCs. It was a very formidable team that faced us. Apart from locking neds up, the big trick for any police officer is overcoming their defence team in court. A good SIO has to examine every strand of evidence: any weakness will be attacked by the defence. You have to ensure that you have covered all the bases. It is a lawyer's job to probe and pick at evidence to see if it can be unravelled and there are times when the defence will produce a thought so unusual that you have not considered it. When you or your officers are in the witness box, it is important to be prepared for the unexpected and, as the saying goes, 'think on your feet'. You need to be sure of your facts and sure of your case at all times.

The trial began with Kevin Drummond, the Advocate Depute, playing the tape-recorded confessions of the accused. He therefore was starting from the same point as we had when we commenced the police investigation. This had never been done before and obviously was a dramatic way to start the trial. I, of course, was not in the court, as I was yet to appear as a witness. As the tapes played and those voices were heard describing the brutal murder of a young man, I was told that a pin dropping would have proved deafening. This set the tone for the coming weeks as more and more dramatic evidence was produced from Scouse, Gayle and his Rastafarian mate. The case blew the lid off the drugs scene in Scotland. Even the press was thunderstruck by the revelations and the fact that there was a drugs link from Clydebank to Bristol. The amount of evidence uncovered in the course of this investigation was phenomenal. At one point during the trial, there were witnesses from Glasgow, Clydebank and, of course, Bristol and they all pointed the finger at the McFadyens and their gang, telling stories of vast amounts of drugs and money changing hands during the course of deals. There were even connections with Spain, Morocco, Florida and the Caribbean Islands.

The evidence from the drug dealers in the witness box clearly unnerved one of the accused. Ricardo Blanco sacked two separate teams of lawyers when he didn't see things going his way and elected instead to conduct his own defence. The court bent over backwards to accommodate Blanco as he was a foreign national and had alleged that he could not read or write in English. A lawyer was appointed to advise him on points of law and he was allowed leeway in court that no qualified lawyer would expect. Some of his comments were at times very abusive towards the witnesses but were also in their own way rather amusing.

Three weeks into the trial, there was further drama when one of the accused, Stephen Mitchell, turned Queen's Evidence and the charges against him were dropped. He then proceeded to testify against his former co-accused. This led to some ructions within court. At one point, he was asked about the hired van used to transport Paul Thorne to his death. Three of the accused had, in fact, gone to hire the van from a firm in the West End of the city. The jury was shown a photograph taken by the manager of the hire company, showing Thomas Currie in the foreground and in the background an excellent profile shot of Ricardo Blanco.

Although the manager had identified Mitchell as being the third man present, Mitchell vehemently denied this in the witness box, saying that the man described by the manager was John Paul McFadyen. This provoked McFadyen to yell from the dock, 'It was you who rented the fucking van, you lying bastard.'

This was all good stuff for the jury to hear. McFadyen's outburst was unique in this case, in that he had refused to make a statement to the police; with this one eruption in open court, he helped confirm his involvement in the crime.

Mitchell's evidence underlined the horror of that dark night on the moors. Under examination by Kevin Drummond, he described how they had driven down to Ayrshire, how they had walked out onto the moors and how Thorne was eventually slain.

'There was a bang,' he told the court. 'I turned round. The guy was lying on the ground.'

Kevin Drummond asked, 'Who had the gun?'

'Ricardo Blanco . . .'

Mitchell then said that Blanco handed the weapon to John Paul McFadyen.

'What did he do?' asked the QC.

'He shot him. He bent over . . .'

'Where did he put the gun to?'

'To his head.'

'How close did he put it?'

'Very close . . .'

The others, Mitchell said, were laughing. Collins was next to pull the trigger, looking away as he did so, then Currie.

When I was eventually called to give evidence, I was in the witness box for a total of three days. I was asked at the start by Kevin Drummond to explain the ins and outs of the investigation from day one. This took some time. Then it was the turn of the defence to question me. The questions from the QCs were cleverly put and what you would expect in the course of a trial, when they are trying to get the best possible result for their client. This was not the case when I was cross-examined by Blanco. It became very personal. I learned that Blanco intended to attack not only my character but also that of my family. I did not have a clue as to what he was up to. It soon became apparent when he started his questions that he had been put up to this by a variety of other criminals in Barlinnie while he was on remand awaiting trial.

First, he referred to my brother John, alleging that John had 'done a runner to Australia, because there was a warrant out for his arrest'. This smear went unchallenged by the court, therefore it was up to me to sort out Blanco and his ridiculous allegations. I said that John had left Glasgow many years before to join the police in Toronto, where he still served as a senior and much-decorated officer. My reply drew quiet smiles from the members of the jury.

During a break in proceedings, a colleague told me that Blanco was going to ask me about locking up a ned called Eddie Bonsai. As far as I could remember I had never locked up any Japanese criminals, so the name meant nothing to me. However when Blanco started this line of questioning and said the name in his Spanish accent, having spoken to him on a number of occasions I understood who he was talking about and managed to turn it to my advantage. He was talking about Edward Burnside, whom I had jailed for drug dealing in Operation Buckfast.

Blanco had met up with Burnside in Barlinnie and during their chats my name had been mentioned. Burnside had told Blanco that he was appealing against his conviction, so he should bring this up in court to help his case – either sour grapes from Burnside or an attempt to wind up Blanco. I am not aware of there ever being any appeal against Burnside's conviction. I'm quite sure that in Barlinnie, Blanco would be seen as fair game and the local hoodlums would have been playing silly buggers with him. Blanco swallowed it hook, line and sinker.

Blanco tried to spar with me verbally over various aspects of evidence, in particular, his involvement in the crime. He tried his best to use his apparent lack of knowledge of the English language and the fact that, as he put it, he was in a foreign country to his advantage. While awaiting trial, he had requested a one-to-one meeting with me. I had cleared this with the Crown Office, to ensure that such a meeting would not jeopardise the case, and was given the go-ahead. I had wondered what Blanco had up his sleeve. In what I saw as an attempt to lessen his own culpability, he offered to carry a tape recorder in Barlinnie in order to get an admission from John Paul McFadyen. However, he had identified a photograph shown to him of Paul Leslie Thorne as being the person he had helped kill on the Fenwick Moors – prior to this identification, we were not aware of the identity of the victim. Blanco brought this up when he was cross-examining me but all he really did was dig himself deeper into the mire.

Donald Findlay acted for Thomas Currie, who had hired the van. His defence was that although he admitted to shooting Thorne, he was the fourth person to do so, the first having been Blanco followed by McFadyen and then Collins. Mitchell had not fired the gun but had, in fact, run off to return with the mattress. Findlay made a great play of this, saying that Currie's shot, being the fourth, could not have killed Thorne, and that his client had, in fact, merely shot a dead body.

I did not agree with this theory because, as the body was never found, there was no possibility of forensics distinguishing which shot had actually been the fatal one. However, Findlay's ploy was a good one and it worked. At the conclusion of the trial, Currie was acquitted on a not-proven verdict. John Paul McFadyen was convicted of murder and nine drug-dealing charges; Ricardo Blanco was convicted of murder; Thomas Collins was convicted of murder and a drug-dealing charge; John Ross McFadyen was convicted of seven drug-dealing charges and received six years' imprisonment. All the men convicted of murder received life sentences, with John Paul McFadyen being sentenced to a total of 46 years.

I can pay no higher tribute to Kevin Drummond than to record the fact that his prosecution was brilliant but, thanks to the hard work of my team, he did have plenty to work with. One of only a handful of murder prosecutions in Scotland without a body, weapon or drugs, this was definitively the most difficult and trying case I ever handled – but very, very satisfying.

Some years later, John Paul McFadyen broke out of prison and caused a stir among those involved in the case, for it was thought that this dangerous man would try to exact some form of revenge. There was talk of police protection for lawyers and witnesses. As it turned out, he headed south but his escape, which was covered extensively by the press, did cause sleepless nights for some people. I was asked to give a talk on this case and while I was speaking on the phone to the man making the invitation, he mentioned McFadyen and the press reports.

'Can't you tell my voice is a bit muffled?' I asked him.

'Why is that?'

'Because I'm speaking to you from under the bed . . .!'

In actual fact, I was not unduly concerned. McFadyen was a dangerous man, sure enough, but he was not stupid enough to come after the cops or the lawyers who put him away. It's all very well for crime fiction writers to come up with that kind of stuff; in real life, it's highly unlikely.

But I found sleeping under my bed not very comfortable, all the same!

Death of a Working Girl

The phone call came in, early one dreich morning in October 1991. A body had been found in Pollok Country Estate Park by a man walking his dog. The dog had run off into the bushes and its owner had stumbled over the dead woman when he chased it. He was naturally pretty shaken by the sight of the battered human body and he immediately went to the Burrell Art Collection buildings nearby to dial 999.

When I arrived at the park around 9 a.m., the crime scene had been disturbed very little, having been visited only by the uniformed officers who had answered the original call. Even they were shaken by what they had seen. When they led me to the location, I could quite understand how they felt. The body was that of a woman who had been beaten so severely that her features were completely unrecognisable. Her face and head had been battered to a bloody pulp, so I was only able to hazard a guess as to her age by her clothing, which suggested she was youngish. The clothing was in oome disarray but did not look as if it had been removed.

The crime scene was secured and the various scene-of-crime experts, a scientist, photographer, fingerprint expert and a pathologist were allowed to conduct examinations while ground searches were being carried out in the immediate area. A police casualty surgeon attended and after a brief consultation with him it was agreed that the age of the dead woman would be late teens to early thirties – we could not be more specific because of the horrific injuries inflicted.

Those injuries had quite clearly been caused by some sort of blunt instrument and, at first, I thought we were looking for a large stone or rock, which would have been to hand in the park during the frenzied attack and left there. Our initial and subsequent searches did not uncover any type of weapon, suggesting that the killer or killers had come prepared. At this stage, we could not say for certain if the murder had occurred here or if the body had simply been dumped in the park. There were bloodstains on the grass around the victim's head but this was to be expected.

Word of murder always gets out and the press had gathered inside the park. Although they are not supposed to, reporters monitored police radio frequencies. They had picked up on the activity in Pollok Park and were expecting some sort of a statement with regard to the police action. It was getting pretty hectic and was about to get even worse.

My private life at the time was as hectic as the fledgling murder probe. September 11 is a memorable date throughout the world because of the terrorist attacks on the World Trade Center in New York. It was already a dreaded date for me, for many years before it was when I married my second wife. It seemed like a good idea at the time; with hindsight, it was a mistake. The one good thing that came out of that particular union was the birth of my son Keith. Over the years, he and I formed a close bond that has never been shaken.

At the time of this murder probe, I was in the middle of trying to negotiate a monetary settlement prior to divorce. This had become pretty messy but my lawyers were working hard on my behalf. Just before I was about to brief the press regarding the murder, I received the news that the lawyers had come up with a settlement agreement they said that with my approval would help conclude matters. This sounded all right, until my lawyer told me that my share would be my training bike and a pair of green Wellington boots. Never one to shilly-shally, I told him to go ahead, as I had more urgent matters to deal with at this precise moment in time. It was one of those days!

I knew the press could be of considerable help in tracing the identity of the dead woman and I issued very sparse details of the events of the morning. These included a description of the clothing she was wearing and her approximate age. I hoped this might jog the memories of anyone close to her. The press were quick to realise that there must be some good reason for my reticence. One journalist asked about the open-ended age limits given but was quickly told to shut it by his more switched-on colleagues, who realised this was due to the state of the body.

As it turned out, we managed to identify the dead woman through police records. Fingerprints taken routinely from the body at the crime scene were quickly compared at the Fingerprint Bureau at headquarters. They revealed that the dead woman was 23-year-old Glasgow prostitute Diane McInally and so the murder investigation was up and running very quickly.

I based my inquiry team at Pollok Police Office, the closest office to the sprawling country park. This was another inquiry in which HOLMES proved a great boon used in conjunction with a dedicated and able staff fully aware of the need to research all information being fed in by outdoor detectives. The computer system allows them to collate and disseminate this information. Ultimately, the senior investigating officer has to make the key decisions regarding the direction of the inquiry and this can only be done if the person leading the inquiry has full trust in his staff, including the outdoor detectives: a good all-round team is essential when dealing with a complicated investigation. A dead prostitute found in the middle of an enormous city park certainly falls into the 'complicated investigation' category.

Where do you start? I had many dealings with prostitutes at various times throughout my career. When I was a younger officer, they had been a great source of information and I found that they were very streetwise and aware of the dangers of their profession. They would probably take a drink or two before starting to ply their trade but generally were on top of their game, so to speak, and aware of what was going on. Older, wiser street girls always looked after each other. Very often, if one of their friends went with a client in his car they would note the car number for safety.

Diane was a single mother with a young son and was very much a Gorbals lass, with her immediate family all based there. Extensive inquiries were required in the area, as the Gorbals was a hotbed of crime, including the sale, supply and consumption of various types of drugs. Diane was an inveterate user of heroin. This was blatantly obvious when her body was examined during the post-mortem examination – her arms and legs were peppered with needle marks and traces of drugs were found in the subsequent blood tests. However, it wasn't the drugs that had killed her – it was the repeated and savage blows to her head.

It appeared she had not been sexually attacked at the time of her death but this did not mean that she had not been sexually active the night before. This was just another avenue for consideration regarding any DNA or other forensic evidence gathered from the body. The circumstances in which the body were found were really not conducive to yielding many scientific clues. Bodies found in open spaces are subject to the vagaries of the weather and various types of contamination. Even over a short period, difficulties can accrue. And Diane's body had been lying out in the rain for some time before she was discovered.

Pollok Police Office may have been the nearest to Pollok Park but it was not the handiest for an inquiry dealing with city prostitutes and their punters. For that, we had to hit 'the Drag'. During the day, the network of hilly streets between Blythswood Square and Waterloo Street in Glasgow's city centre is a busy commercial district peppered with office blocks and teeming with clerical workers. By night, it becomes something else. Instead of workers doing business, you have street girls doing the business. Instead of office workers standing on the pavements having cigarette breaks, you have prostitutes offering oral satisfaction of another kind. The ironic thing is that all this illicit behaviour goes on a stone's throw from police headquarters in Pitt Street. The afternoon of the first day of the inquiry, I had a police incident caravan placed at Pitt Street and its junction with Waterloo Street. Three officers staffed this, with a team of detectives ready to hit the Drag that first night. I thought that if we could catch the prostitutes quickly then they would be able to assist us in tracking Diane's movements. The murder had been well covered by the media and would be the main topic of conversation that night.

The idea was to get the detectives on the streets from 7 p.m. until the early hours of the morning to speak to as many of the girls as possible. The red-light district is part of 'A' Division, which covers Glasgow city centre and at that time had a Vice Squad, which dealt exclusively with the prostitutes and their clients. The assistance from these officers was to prove invaluable as the inquiry progressed.

Many steps were taken and put in place on this first day of the inquiry, and at about 8 p.m. I was just about to have my first cup of tea that day when in walked our new chief constable, Leslie Sharp. This was the first time I had met this gentleman. Mr Sharp had been with the Metropolitan Police in London for much of his career, mostly as a working detective. The word coming back from other senior officers who had met him was that he knew what he was about regarding proper police work.

Mr Sharp accepted my offer of a mug of tea and sat down to discuss the day's events. He obviously knew how hard this type of investigation could be and his succinct remark was, 'You need an inquiry like this

195

like you need a hole in your head.' I took an instant liking to the man. He went on say that I could have any resources I needed during the inquiry. This was most unusual. Generally during major inquiries, you were continually being asked to keep spending to a minimum. I took no notice of the penny-pinchers: my main concern was always to solve the crime and bugger the cost. Mr Sharp was not aware of my usual techniques but his offer was much appreciated.

It started to become obvious that this inquiry would be a drag in every sense of the word. Many murder investigations are difficult and cases involving murdered prostitutes are often slow to solve. This proved to be so with the McInally case. Officers worked 12-hour shifts, talking to working girls, tracking down punters, hitting dead ends because prostitution is, by necessity, a clandestine trade. A murder probe is fuelled by information and the customers of prostitutes are seldom keen to come forward and talk. Nevertheless, the statements taken began to paint a dreadful picture of the prostitute population of Glasgow.

Diane McInally had a pretty god-awful lifestyle that centred on her work as a prostitute and her need for drugs. However, she cared very much for her young son and was, as far as she could be, a caring mother who ensured that the child was properly looked after while she was out on the Drag.

My hopes that the girls on the Drag would be of help proved pretty wide of the mark. I learned that there was almost a two-shift system, with some of the older girls coming out earlier to catch the punters who wanted sex after work before going home to the wife and kiddies. Lots of these women had worked these streets for many years and were more than happy to cooperate with the police, especially in the context of a prostitute murder, but few of them knew Diane, who apparently worked the later shift.

Late-shift prostitutes were invariably younger and hooked on drugs, and these were the types of girls with whom Diane associated. Most people can cast their minds back over the previous 24 hours without much of a problem but when you are dealing with drug-addled prostitutes who quite honestly don't know if it's New Year or New York, you really have a big problem. These girl junkies were far more reluctant to speak to my officers than the older ones and both age groups were inclined to give false names and addresses. As they were wandering about the area regularly, and being interviewed by different officers, it began to become quite confusing. A system was devised where they were invited back to the police caravan, where they were given a cup of tea – which they gladly accepted, as the nights were cold – and their statements would be taken there. We would also ask them if they would mind if we took a couple of photographs for future reference in the inquiry, stressing these were not for inclusion in their files in the Scottish Criminal Records Office. By and large, they agreed to this. This enabled us to fit a number of names to faces or, on many occasions, several names to the one face. From this long, tiring but very necessary process, a picture began to emerge of the current activities of the prostitutes and the drug scene in that area of the city. The walls of the caravan began to look like the modern-art section of an art gallery.

At Pollok, statements from the street girls and the Gorbals were being fed into the computer. It started to become clear that Diane was not only a user of heroin but could well have been involved in the supply of drugs to the girls on the Drag. This opened up a range of possibilities regarding motive and needed to be explored – but very gently, as there was still a lot of grieving over her death among her family and the other street girls.

The drugs being used by the street girls ranged from heroin and temazepam to cocaine and cannabis, depending on what they could afford and what was available. The girls' brains were scrambled because of drug abuse. Clear and concise statements were not easy to come by. They didn't necessarily know the proper names of the girls whom they worked beside every night, so the photographs were invaluable. I had a small room set aside at Pollok, which I used for the duplicate photographs taken of the prostitutes in order that we had a good cross reference system going with their various names and aliases listed. This room was permanently locked to keep out rubbernecks and was available for viewing on a 'need to know' basis. You do get people being over-inquisitive – even in Police Offices!

At this time, Strathclyde Police was receiving its annual visit from Her Majesty's Force Inspectorate, in the shape of Sir Colin Samson, an elderly English gentleman whose overall task was to examine all forces throughout the British Isles to ensure they maintained the highest standards possible. He had decided that he wished to view a major football match and an ongoing major inquiry. He was fortunate enough to have scheduled his visit at a time when Celtic were having a good European run, so he intended taking in a midweek match. Before attending it, he accompanied Assistant Chief Constable Steve Mannion on a visit to my inquiry at Pollok Office. When they arrived, I briefed them on the details of the investigation then took them on a tour of the various rooms and told them of their purpose. Sir Colin then, surprisingly, asked if I had a wee private room attached to the inquiry. I thought, 'He has done his homework before coming here.' I duly opened up the room containing the photographs of the working prostitutes. I, of course, had made many visits to the caravan and the Drag during the inquiry and was aware of the procedure regarding the taking of photographs, which were generally head-and-shoulders shots of the subject. One time, an old lady in a long coat and winter boots and wearing a headscarf appeared at the caravan. She said that she was a prostitute and worked the Drag, and insisted on a cup of tea and having her photograph taken. It was a quiet night, so we duly obliged but took a full-length shot, which was included in our whore's gallery.

Sir Colin Samson and Steve Mannion were quite astounded by the amount of effort being expended to solve this crime and uncover the prostitute network. Sir Colin asked about the various names and aliases they used, then his eyes were drawn to the photograph of the old woman and he asked if she was a prostitute – so I told him what had occurred. He then asked if she had got many punters that night. I said I had asked her the same question but she had said no. I had, in fact, asked her if she had ever had any punters at any time and she had replied, 'No, son, but I keep trying, I keep trying.' Sir Colin had a hard time trying not to laugh and nearly choked on his mug of tea. I drew a disapproving look from Mr Mannion. I hope Sir Colin enjoyed the football as much as he seemed to enjoy his visit to Pollok. They were both fine gentlemen. I was delighted when his inspection report for Strathclyde positively commented on my inquiry and the morale of the team working on it.

I did not mind that particular visit; however, many other times when I was conducting a major inquiry – we always seemed to have a major inquiry running in 'G' Division – higher-ranking officers dropped in simply to pass the time of day. Often, they had no idea how to solve a serious crime. It was like politicians visiting a disaster site. It was just a bloody nuisance, especially if they started asking inane questions and making suggestions as to how you might solve the case. They really pissed me off.

However, the Diane McInally case was dragging on. We were in the third week of the inquiry by this time and not much seemed to be progressing from all our efforts. The first 48 hours may be the most important in any murder inquiry but you must maintain your focus in the long-haul cases. And we were about to make a breakthrough.

One nickname had shown in two recent statements taken in the Gorbals. A man known as 'Dagger' was an apparent associate of Diane McInally. He was supposed to be involved in the drug trade but this nickname was not registering on any police file. I had detectives working full-time on the Gorbals connection to trace 'Dagger'. He turned out to be a 20-year-old ned from Yoker. His actual name was Dale Clark but he was referred to by friends and acquaintances as 'Daga'. He was also known to the prostitutes as 'The Egg Man'; they met him at the end of their working day in Dunkin Donuts, an all-night, fast-food restaurant at the corner of Union Street and Argyle Street. This 'Egg Man' tag was a term I had never heard before, except in the context of someone who delivered dairy produce – or in The Beatles song 'I Am the Walrus'. Clark's 'Egg Man' nickname, though, referred to his illicit trade in temazepam capsules, known as eggs or jellies. These are heavy sleeping pills, generally prescribed by a doctor and taken in doses of one or two at a time. Many of the prostitutes, due to their drug habits and tolerance levels, would literally swallow them by the handful at the end of their day on the Drag or withdraw the liquid from the capsules and inject it in the hope of a quicker or better hit.

It appeared that Diane's usual day consisted of seeing her child off to school; after school, he would go to his grandmother's house. In the afternoon, Diane would visit her junkie friends and they would shoot up, filling their veins full of heroin to put them into a comatose state; they called this 'cabbaging'. When she had recovered somewhat from this condition, she would get herself ready to go on the Drag as a prostitute and, as it turned out, perhaps even as a pusher. She had a house in the Queen Elizabeth Square flats, a haven for junkies. The entrance was covered by video cameras and from this we recovered a sighting of Diane at around 9 p.m. as she left for work that night on her own.

We had been told Clark had been seen speaking to Diane up the Drag on the night of her murder but this information was very vague. It suggested that they both had gone to a flat near to the Argyle Street bus depot. Junkies knew this flat as the local shooting alley, a place where they could go for a fix. It had been suggested that Diane was selling drugs supplied by Daga, so this was another possible connection for the two – and a connection well worth exploring.

I had Clark brought to Pollok. A statement was taken from him by the two detectives who brought him in. He had several previous convictions for drug abuse and dealing and also had form for petty thefts. Although a small-time criminal, he had been around the block a few times and knew the procedures when being interviewed by the police. He gave a very vague statement with regard to his movements on the night in question. It was some time ago, he said, and his memory wasn't too good. Being a heroin user made him pretty fuzzy about most of his actions and his whereabouts. This was just the start; his statement had to be fully checked in all its aspects.

His mother, with whom he lived, also had to be interviewed regarding his habits and his lifestyle around the home. It is always necessary to build up a complete picture of someone's typical behaviour so that you can identify anything that is out of the ordinary. His mother was not aware of what her son did in his time away from home. She could tell us that occasionally he would come home and throw all of his clothing, plus trainers, into the washing machine, which she never questioned as she never knew what kind of mood he would be in. We were very interested to hear this but she could not be specific about the last time it had happened. If we could have tied this behaviour to the night Diane was murdered, this would have been very significant but we could not. It was only a pointer but it put Clark into the suspect category in my mind.

By now, it was early December. Almost two full months had passed. We had interviewed and re-interviewed the prostitutes but were learning very little. One, who also hailed from the Gorbals, insisted that she and Diane had spent the afternoon together, both injecting heroin. She said they had left the flat to go up the Drag at the same time (the video evidence from the camera at the flats had already shown that Diane had left alone). She also said that she had been with Diane at their stance in Waterloo Street, but other prostitutes said that they had seen Diane on her own and generally they classed this woman as a romancer known for making up stories, who was talking rubbish as usual. But we had to look into every possible lead. The detectives dealing with her were at their wits' end with the different information she kept coming up with, which was perhaps not surprising as her drug addiction had her totally spaced out. We eventually asked if she would see a qualified hypnotist, to which she readily agreed. We wanted to try to separate fact from fiction in her scrambled brain. During such inquiries, there is always

the hope that you will turn up a star witness. However, sometimes
you find someone who likes the limelight and will go over the score
trying to be more than helpful. You must be very careful of these
types, as they can throw an inquiry completely off track.

The hypnotist was contacted and we arranged a consultation at
Pollok Police Office to be overseen by a procurator fiscal. After the
session, which took place in the early evening, we were none the wiser.
The hypnotist came out of the consultation totally bemused and in
need of a good malt whisky. He could make neither head nor tail of
this woman. She really could not be believed and was a total enigma
– a headbanger, as we say in Glasgow!

The 'A' Division Vice Squad had come up with the registration
numbers of in excess of 300 cars that were regularly spotted cruising
the Drag. Cars were checked only if thought to belong to the most
frequent punters. The drivers of these vehicles had been asked to
come forward and speak to us in confidence but this did not have
much effect. It would have required many more staff than had been
allocated to me if we had to go and trace every car but I had considered
this problem and how best to deal with it.

I had bided my time, hoping that other lines of inquiry would
reveal who had murdered Diane, but as the festive season grew closer
I decided to make my own Christmas broadcast, one which was not
of good cheer and glad tidings to all men. I set up interviews with
the media and newspapers, announcing that my team would not be
having time off over the festive season – we would be visiting the
homes of car owners who had regularly been seen on the Drag. I
emphasised that this would be taking place over the Christmas period,
when these men were at home with their families.

I hoped this slightly dramatic line of attack would hit home. I was
looking for a reasonable turnout to my request that if these men came
to my Incident Room at Pollok Police Office of their own accord,
their statements would be treated in the strictest confidence and their
homes would not be visited. I was totally amazed when about 500 men

showed up and admitted using their cars to have sex with prostitutes on the Drag. We had bigger queues than the high street stores. It was astonishing to see how many upstanding members of society turned up – everyone from sheriffs to ministers of the Kirk. And it helped to clear up that part of the inquiry in double-quick time.

With well over a thousand statements on HOLMES, we set up a separate room containing another four monitor screens, which I operated with my Detective Chief Inspector and two detective inspectors. We often sat long into the night poring over these statements, pinpointing those needing further clarification or investigation, discounting others that were of no further value to the inquiry. This was a tedious but totally necessary job; although our Incident Room staff had already checked these statements, they all had to be seen and signed off by the senior investigating officer or his deputies to ensure complete control. I was also still making nightly trips to the Drag to ensure that nothing was being missed. In an inquiry such as this, attention to detail is vitally important; all incoming data has to be constantly checked and re-checked.

Dale Clark was still in the frame. For all that the information regarding him was pretty thin, it was not to be ignored, and further inquiries regarding his activities were continuing. We learned he did not work alone. Small-time he may have been but he had other partners in his drug-dealing business and they were pretty violent types who would certainly have been capable of inflicting serious damage on anyone who did not toe the line.

I had Clark brought back to Pollok Police Office for a further interview by the officers who had been probing his background. Various other points were put to him that we had learned during the investigation. Clark did not admit anything other than knowing Diane very well. I was not happy with this straight denial. He was a junkie. He was a known crook. He was a drug dealer. He was known to prostitutes as a supplier. He had some fairly heavy connections. Something was wrong. Clark was not a strong character; he was not long out of prison and apparently when inside kept himself in good shape by gym work, but physical shape does not relate to mental capability, especially in a heavy drug abuser. After the interview by the other detectives, I decided I would have a crack at him. Of course, all of the detectives had discussed the previous interview at length to see if there were any obvious chinks in his defensive armour we could exploit. We were not under any time constraints as he had agreed to come voluntarily to the office. So I began to play little mind games with him, talking of his friendship with Diane and how it had come about, asking whether it was a sexual relationship or purely business, enquiring if he had liked Diane as a person or merely as someone to be exploited. His view was that it was all one and the same thing – such was the world they lived in. Talking to him was a stomach-churning, but necessary, learning process.

Once I had gained his confidence slightly, the talk started to flow a bit more freely. He relaxed but was always on his guard, which was unusual: a drug addict generally very wound up and ready for their next fix looks for a friend. He seemed to be able to keep the lid on his feelings even though I was placing him under a tremendous amount of mental pressure. There had to be a reason for this but I couldn't figure it out. He seemed almost ready to burst but he didn't. I didn't have enough to charge him without more evidence, so we let him go.

I seemed to have reached a stalemate. I was convinced of Clark's involvement and could link him to Diane and her various activities. However, thanks to the lack of good-quality evidence from the drug-addled prostitutes and the victim's other dubious junkie friends, I was struggling. My team and I were not going to give up, though. We were going to continue to push hard in all directions, explore every avenue – including information coming from the criminal community.

An inmate of Barlinnie Prison had claimed that another prisoner had been mouthing off about Diane's murder. The informer was from the south side of Glasgow and was aware of the hunt for Diane's killer. His information put a different slant on things: he alleged that there had been two men involved in the murder. This prisoner was perfectly prepared to give a statement about what the other prisoner had said, which took real courage, as the person he was referring to was a dangerous criminal known for his violent behaviour who had been accused but cleared at trial of a particularly horrific murder case in the north side of the city some years earlier.

Our informant alleged that Clark and his sidekick were involved in supplying drugs to prostitutes through Diane McInally. She had not only used the product herself but committed the cardinal sin of spending the proceeds and not passing the cash to her suppliers. The resultant confrontation ended in her death.

Clark's sidekick was serving time for a series of crimes, for which he had been fired in by his girlfriend after Diane's death. Generally, nobody grassed on him but getting him locked up for smaller crimes kept him away from the McInally investigation and may have been a very clever move.

The evidence regarding the close involvement of Clark with Diane and his association with the Barlinnie prisoner and his loose talk in the jail was starting to give us a clearer picture of what had probably happened on the night of the murder. It was looking less as if she had been killed by a punter, more as if she had been removed by two of her partners in drug crime.

Accompanied by Detective Inspector Ian McAllister, I presented a full report on the circumstances surrounding the murder to two senior fiscals. I requested that I be allowed to bring the prisoner from Barlinnie on a Fiscal's release in order that I could question him and charge him and Clark with the murder of Diane McInally. I felt there was more than sufficient evidence to bring these two to trial and at the time the Fiscals appeared to agree with me. The following day, I had Clark arrested and brought to Pollok Police Office. The prisoner was brought from Barlinnie but the Fiscal's release stipulated that the order was only for the purpose of charging and no questioning was to take place at this stage.

Both men were brought together in an interview room in order to record the caution and charge. Neither man made any reply while the tape was running. Once the tape had stopped, the prisoner's pent-up fury gave way to a mouthful of expletives directed at me. The prisoner was carted back to Barlinnie and Clark was incarcerated at Pollok Police Office until their initial court appearance the following day.

Next morning, I was out of the office on personal business when DI McAllister phoned me to tell me that Clark had been liberated by the Procurator Fiscal. I returned to the office to find a letter addressed to me from the Senior Procurator Fiscal Depute – one of the men with whom I had spoken – informing me that he considered there was insufficient evidence to justify proceedings against the accused meantime. This seemed to be a complete reversal of what I had understood from our previous discussion. Because of the terms of the Fiscal's release, I had even been prevented from interviewing the prisoner regarding his alleged involvement in the crime. The Fiscal's actions took me completely by surprise and I was not privy to the reasons for his decision.

The investigation of the murder of Diane McInally had turned into a travesty for her family. Reluctance of the Crown to bring those two men to trial has ensured that they have not yet been afforded any closure on this dreadful murder. She was no angel – a prostitute, drug addict and dealer – but she was also a single mum who loved her child. She did not deserve to die a brutal death like this. I believe to this day that we had the right men in the frame for the killing. We had no forensic evidence but we had a strong, if circumstantial case. I believe, given time, Dale Clark would have burst and confessed his involvement. His sidekick might have been a harder nut to crack.

Dale Clark is now dead, having succumbed to a drugs overdose. Since this case, the other man has been convicted of the culpable homicide of another heroin addict from the Gorbals who had been paying attention to his girlfriend.

The Final Years

Strathclyde Police leased a helicopter from a commercial operator in 1990. The American-made Bell Jet Ranger was the first resource of its kind in Scotland – although such aircraft had been in use in England for some time – and was a tremendous additional arm for the force. It was used as a means of fast response to incidents, as a backup during pursuit and, latterly, to assist with reporting on traffic problems.

When the idea of an 'eye in the sky' was first suggested, some officers thought that our chief constable was playing a game of one-upmanship with his fellow Scottish chief constables and that perhaps the idea had not been properly thought through. I believe, however, that the concept was sound, but the transition to actual practice was not well enough thought out. This, in my opinion, was highlighted tragically in the opening weeks of 1990.

On 24 January, while still in its early days of use and in the teeth of a raging blizzard, the helicopter crashed into a block of old people's flats. Sergeant Malcolm Herd, who was 30 years old and a father of four, died in the tragedy. His crew, another sergeant, a police inspector and a civilian pilot, were all injured and were lucky to escape with their lives. Fortunately, none of the residents of the flats were hurt.

That dismal, snowy midday, I had just left the office to go for lunch when I received a phone call from one my detective inspectors, telling me about the disaster at Eastwood Toll on the south side of the city. It was all hands to the pumps, so I headed for the crash site. Several other senior officers, including the divisional commander, were also on their way to take control of the incident.

When I arrived, I was stunned to see a senior police officer directing traffic at the roundabout while other officers of lesser rank scrambled about near the crashed helicopter. Something did not seem quite right. To my mind, there seemed to be no proper police coordination.

The aircraft had crashed into the side of a block of flats situated on the north side of the roundabout and finished up in a crumpled mess in the gardens below. It struck the building then slid down the side, where it had come to rest at the base. The ambulance service had responded as quickly as possible and had removed the crew to hospital. I learned that one of the sergeants had been killed, while the rest of the crew had sustained serious injuries.

I was quickly appointed senior investigating officer. It was immediately apparent to me that this was going to be a massive inquiry and so I put the wheels in motion to have a squad of detectives and a HOLMES Room set up at Giffnock Police Office as soon as possible.

Another senior officer from Giffnock, on his own initiative, had cleared the building of its elderly inhabitants. He knew it was the thing to be done and he did an extremely good and essential job. Once he had completed that task, he asked for further instructions. He, too, was surprised that they were not immediately forthcoming.

Several questions were being asked by officers of high rank: assistant chief constables, for instance, who had attended at the scene were concerned about their own input regarding the acquisition of the helicopter and wondering if they were in any way to blame. I was asked if I thought that the helicopter should have been flying that day in such dreadful conditions. My response to this question was to ask another one: 'Well, are the motorcyclists out in this weather?' I knew full well the response would be 'Of course not.' Traffic Department heads had a responsibility to give instructions in respect of dangerous road and weather conditions to their officers, as I would to mine if they were going into any dangerous situations. The helicopter came under the control of the Traffic Department but flying conditions were unknown territory for officers more used to keeping their wheels on the ground, and pilots would seek information from Air Traffic Control about the weather conditions.

This investigation began with many senior officers wondering what my method of inquiry would lead to and how I would be apportioning any blame. Such an inquiry is just like any other – you start by talking to people. Witnesses who had been close to the crash scene had to be interviewed in order to build up a picture of what had happened. This needed to be done quickly and I realised I needed additional, experienced detectives to get the job done. As well as using my own team, I also called in members of the Serious Crime Squad.

First, we needed to know why the helicopter had been in the air. A simple call to Force Control at headquarters told us the helicopter had scrambled in response to a radio shout to help find a getaway car used in a robbery in Paisley. The vehicle had last been spotted heading over an area known as Barrhead Dams and Force Control had asked the crew to head over there to see if they could spot it.

The pilot was no callow youth. He was an experienced flyer who had served with the Armed Forces. Once up in the air, it appears that because of the atrocious weather conditions the crew had decided to call off the search in the Barrhead Dams and return to base, a helipad on the north side of the River Clyde. This aircraft had no radar navigational assistance and so the pilot had navigated by landmarks. Due to the horrendous weather, he was apparently trying to follow the A77 – the main road that cuts through Glasgow from the city centre to Ayrshire – back towards the city, to its base and safety.

This turned out to be a dangerous decision. There are fields and golf courses in and around leafy Newton Mearns on which I am quite sure an experienced pilot could have safely landed and waited for better weather conditions. A member of the public had actually witnessed the helicopter before the crash, about to touch down in a field behind his house. However, the pilot veered off again, seemingly having decided to try to make it back to base. Perhaps there was something wrong with that choice of landing site. Perhaps he still believed he could make it.

Shortly afterwards, during an attempt at an emergency landing, the helicopter hit the block of flats at Eastwood Toll. The Jet Ranger made a steep left turn before a rotor tip hit a wall protruding from the flats at 70 ft. It fell 45 ft before crashing into the side of the building and then plummeted in two sections to the ground. This was confirmed later in a report by the Air Accidents Investigation Branch.

Each machine has from the time of its inception a logbook, which stays with the craft no matter how many times it changes owner, and this logbook details all upgrades to the craft. The owners are also notified by the parent company of any changes or modifications necessary, especially in relation to weather conditions in which the helicopter may be used. It had been discovered that in severe, snowy weather, it was deemed essential to fit snow baffles in front of the exhaust intakes to prevent snow clogging up the forward air filters and thus preventing the jet engine from functioning properly – apparently, that's what caused this aircraft's engines to fail. It seems clear to me that this simple and non-expensive procedure should have been carried out on the 19-year-old helicopter, especially as it was required to operate in Scottish winter weather.

As officer in charge of the inquiry, I attended the post-mortem examination of the fatally injured sergeant, who had sustained severe head injuries. The pathologist described the injuries as being similar to that of a motorcyclist who had not been wearing a helmet. I asked if the sergeant had been wearing proper headgear could this have had an impact on the seriousness of the injuries. The surgeon agreed that undoubtedly it would have.

The inquiry showed that the police crew was really not properly equipped for their role. Not only did they lack protective headgear, they also did not have flame-retardant clothing. They wore normal police uniform.

My continuing inquiries showed that when there is a helicopter crash, the craft generally bursts into flames as it hits the ground, with the hot engine igniting the fuel. Indeed, an ex-pilot from the Air Accidents Investigation Branch arrived to conduct inquiries on their behalf and confirmed this. He was extremely helpful to the police investigation and was able to assist greatly with information that was not readily available to a police force. Flame-retardant clothing was essential and should have been supplied for all police crew. Incidentally, the lack of proper gear was not only restricted to the unfortunate crew. When the scene-of-crime photographer Ray Eddie arrived to record the scene on film, he found himself gracing the pages of the *Daily Record* wearing a black bin bag over his own winter clothing in an attempt to protect himself from the elements. Unbelievably, he was criticised by senior officers for kitting himself out in such a manner!

It was extremely fortunate that this crash had not resulted in a fire. Luckily, the fuel spilled into a basement entrance, away from the hot engines. The wild, cold weather helped in that it cooled the engines and prevented fuel from igniting; otherwise, there might well have been other deaths due to fire.

The sergeant who survived the crash was thrown away from the helicopter and came-to sitting on the basement steps of the flats.

He had been in the rear seat beside the sergeant who was killed and was soaked with fuel. Despite having a broken arm and suffering from shock, he was aware enough to put some distance between himself and the crashed machine, because he knew it could explode at any second. He was found later on a nearby wall. The pilot and the inspector who were sitting at the front of the aircraft were both unconscious and had to be pulled free by emergency teams.

A Fatal Accident Inquiry was held in Paisley later that year and concluded that 'protective helmets and flameproof flying suits and boots should be worn by all persons flying in helicopters on police air support operations', and that the helicopter leasing company should 'revise their operations manual so as to express in clear and consistent terms their policy that flying should not take place in snow and the action to be taken if snow is encountered in flight'.

Due to lessons learned during that very unfortunate incident, successive police crew members have been properly equipped and much more attention has since been paid to their safety.

Perhaps, though, if such attention had been paid at the time, a young sergeant's life might have been saved.

THE USE OF THE MEDIA

Any investigation of serious crime invariably catches the attention of the ladies and gentlemen of the news media. Sometimes, this can be of great assistance; at others it's a bloody nuisance. However, it is necessary to learn how to deal with the various reporters, as the press can be a powerful tool, if used properly. Getting to know the personalities involved is a great help. Most reporters are straightforward people doing their best to report a given incident as factually as possible. But you do come across some who are always pushing for another angle and trying to sensationalise an already pretty graphic or gruesome event. Learning who you can trust and who you cannot is often a painful experience for cops. Sometimes, when you are in charge of high-profile inquiries, particularly when it involves something potentially salacious, the media will be all over you right from the start and you must be very careful regarding your quotes.

On one occasion I was leading an inquiry that had to do with the sodomising of young teenage boys. Three had already been attacked near to a railway line in the Pollok district and I decided to call a press conference. I had some pretty good leads and was certain that we would catch the person responsible but, until then, I did not want another boy being attacked. I thought that by letting the public know, the attacker would lie low and, until we nabbed him, children would be safe.

The press conference consisted of all the usual suspects from the *Daily Record*, the *Sun*, the *Herald* and the *Daily Mail*, plus local newspapers and a young lad from Radio Scotland. Calling a conference gives you the advantage of having your script prepared. Reporters, however, can be like lawyers in trying to catch you off guard and attempting to make you dramatise crimes even further. One piped up, 'Is this man liable to kill the next one?'

I batted it straight back at him asking, 'Are these crimes not bad enough for you?' He never repeated the question. The young lad from the radio asked for a tape-recorded interview after the conference. He was silly enough to repeat the murder question. I told him in graphic language, which I knew could not be broadcast, not to be as bloody stupid as that old hack.

Nevertheless, the object of the exercise was achieved and within four days we had locked up a horrible creature named James Aries for the series of sex attacks on young boys. He appeared at the Glasgow High Court where he was sentenced to seven years for his crimes.

NEARLY A BIG MISTAKE

The role of the nightwatchman used to be quite a mundane occupation in our society, sometimes being handed to retired gentlemen who would sit in their little huts drinking endless cups of tea and doing crossword puzzles to while away the dreary hours while occasionally taking a walk around their domain.

This has changed in recent times with the growth in the number of 'security' firms. There are, of course, many decent security firms performing a reasonable function – but I stress the word reasonable, as some of the firms in the west of Scotland operate on a wing and a prayer, and there have been many instances of trouble between rival firms. The word 'protection' has taken on a sinister new meaning as some ruthless individuals have muscled in on the industry. You can also find animosity brewing between the staff of the same company and this is not surprising when you consider the calibre of staff sometimes employed, which has switched to rough characters, including people with criminal backgrounds.

One weekend in the early 1990s, I decided to take some time out and have a pleasant walking break. I booked into a country hotel near Fort William and, after a long, strenuous walk I was relaxing in the hotel's jacuzzi when a member of staff told me that I was required on the phone. It was a call from my office. I could have gladly strangled that member of staff but my cops knew not to bother me unless it was really urgent, so I knew there had to be a problem requiring my attention.

On the other end of the line was Detective Inspector Willie Dow, one of my best officers and a close friend whose judgement and ability I never doubted. We had worked on many inquiries together and trusted each other implicitly. He filled me in regarding the situation.

'There's been a murder in Pollok,' he said. 'Body of a security guard, off the Barrhead Road. Middle-aged guy. It's a nasty one, Joe.'

'How'd he die?'

'Beaten to death, looks like.'

That was it – I knew it was the end of my break. Crime is crime whatever it is but murder takes priority.

'Get the ball rolling, Willie,' I said. 'I'll be back as soon as I can.'

While I drove back to Glasgow, the post-mortem was taking place. This revealed that the guard had been severely beaten about the head, causing numerous fractures. His manager had arrived on site about 10 a.m. when he could not raise the guard on the radio. He found him lying face down in a muddy pool. The pathologist found water in his lungs. This meant he had still been alive after the attack and had been left to drown.

The site, on the outskirts of Pollok, was pretty isolated. It was part of an old farm towards Pollok Estate and had no surrounding houses, therefore the guard was totally on his own. Whatever had taken place was unlikely to have been witnessed. The starting point was the security firm and whether rivals had levelled threats at this particular site or any other. There was nothing of value to be stolen, as it was only in the initial construction stages. The foundations had just been excavated and, basically, it was just a big muddy field with some large concrete drainage pipes in evidence and nothing much else, surrounded by a rather makeshift, six-foot-high chicken-wire fence.

So what was the motive? The dead man's clothing was checked and all of his possessions including his wallet were there. This, of course, was checked with his relatives – not a pleasant task but it had to be done. Nothing was missing from his hut, so again – why the murder?

Normally, we would start looking into other aspects of the dead man's life, but early on in this inquiry we concentrated our efforts on the security firm, who appeared to be rather reticent in speaking to the CID. They were quickly put in their place and information started to come out regarding certain practices.

By now, it was Monday and things were beginning to shape up. This company turned out to be a rather rough-and-ready outfit and our inquiries began to reveal to us what had actually been taking place between their employees. Money was the name of the game and various employees had had squabbles over the distribution of weekend overtime. A guard would spend more or less all weekend on site receiving £3 per hour for an 18-hour shift. The dead man had, in fact, been allocated the Pollok site in preference to another guard. Whether this was to do with favouritism, either man's standard of work, or a pay-off to the foreman was never properly established. Our investigation, however, showed that on the Friday night prior to the murder, the guard who had first been offered the shift had been caught on CCTV, threatening his foreman with a pickaxe handle. The threats had taken place in a car park and the offending guard was quite clearly identifiable and behaving totally irrationally. This behaviour, coupled with his obvious rancour at not getting the shift that had been given to the dead guard, made him our number one suspect.

On Tuesday morning, I had him brought to Pollok Police Office. It is always a tense time when you send your troops to pick up a murder suspect. If suspects get wind of your intentions, they will generally be off on their toes. The word came back, though, that this man had been captured in his home in Castlemilk. When he was brought in, he was a quivering wreck who admitted to a severe drink problem. Two of my officers began the interview, which was tape-recorded. He admitted everything regarding threatening his foreman with a pickaxe handle and explained it was regarding overtime and bad feelings between them.

However, when it came to any suggestions about his involvement in the murder, he would not have it. He said that on Saturday night he had been at home, playing cards with two of his friends. He readily gave us their names. Officers were dispatched to bring them to the office but we could see the usual cover-up and staged alibi in the offing. This was always to be expected when dealing with Glasgow neds.

We got a bit of a surprise, however. His pals certainly backed up his story about the card game and the drinking session that went along with it. But they also said that around midnight, our suspect had become angrier and angrier as he thought about how he should have been out earning money. Shortly after midnight, he told them that he was 'going to sort this out' and he had left them to their card game and their drinking. His friends said they stayed in his house till about 2 a.m. and he still had not returned.

It was not looking good for our suspect. We had detained him at 8 a.m. and legislation in those days allowed us to hold him for six hours without any access to a lawyer. The one phone call by the suspect is a myth perpetuated by TV and certainly does not happen in Scotland. If a suspect requires a lawyer, then one will be contacted by the police and will be told when they can see their client. Some solicitors will certainly try to overcome this legislation by appearing at a police office and attempting to bluster and intimidate officers into bending this rule. This didn't wash in Pollok. We had six hours to talk to this man. I fully expected my interviewing officers to come to me within an hour or so with a full taped confession telling us how he had visited the building site and had a set-to with the other guard which had led to a fight resulting in the death. Not everything goes to plan, however, and although our suspect was in a right emotional state, he would not admit to the murder.

He had been in custody for two hours and still there was no admission. Time was wearing on, so I decided I would speak to him. I was sure that he was ready to tell us the truth, as the evidence against him seemed overwhelming. I faced him across the scarred wooden table, the double-headed tape recorder beside us whirring away, and outlined the case we had against him.

'We know you left the house that night,' I said. 'Your pals told us . . .'

'Aye, I did,' he said, 'but I never went anywhere near that site.'

'Where did you go then?'

'Just went for a walk, an' that. To try and cool down, like.'

'Did you visit any other site?'

'No.'

'Maybe looking for the foreman . . .'

'No.'

'. . . to pick up the argument where it left off.'

'No.'

'You were pretty angry.'

'Aye, but I never touched nobody. I never did it. I never killed that guy.'

With the evidence stacked up against him, there certainly was enough to charge him but I still had over two hours left before the time limit ran out, so I suggested to my team that we should have an early lunch and mull over the case. Something did not sit right with me. I certainly had had other murder cases where the accused had not admitted their guilt but this one seemed different.

Call it providence but as we were eating our Greggs bridies, Detective Sergeant George Lambie came bursting into the detective inspectors' room in a state of high excitement. He had just taken a phone call from a lady who stayed in a slightly isolated farm cottage near the building site. She and her husband had been interviewed on the Sunday afternoon but had not supplied any useful information. It appears that the detective sergeant who had interviewed the couple had failed to ask if there were any other people living in their home. As it turned out, this was a serious oversight!

This lady had said in her phone call to George Lambie that she had never mentioned or been asked about other occupants by the interviewing officer but that she and her husband had taken in a lodger about two weeks before the murder. She went further, to say that on the night in question this man had arrived home very late and when she had gone into her bathroom the next morning she had found his muddy clothes steeping in a bath full of water. He had told her that he had slipped on his way home. Having read newspaper reports on the killing, she had decided to let us know about it.

As soon as I heard this, alarm bells started ringing. George had been told that the lodger was presently at work. He was a barman in The

39 Steps, close to Glasgow Central railway station. I told George to gather up a squad and head for this pub. I wanted the lodger brought to Pollok right away, as time was growing short. We only had another hour to charge our first suspect – in effect put up, or shut up. It was going to be extremely tight. George drove like a bat out of hell and luckily the guy was serving behind the bar when he entered the premises. He was brought to Pollok.

Things were quite stressful. We already had in custody someone who pushed all the right buttons for being charged with a murder. However, this new turn of events really caused lots of problems. The only way I could think my way out of this was to immediately interview the barman in the detective inspectors' room. I put to him what we had learned from his landlady regarding his activities on Saturday night and Sunday morning. He told me that he had left the bar early on Sunday morning rather the worse for drink. He had managed to get a taxi to drop him off at Barrhead Road. He was, he admitted, totally pissed and definitely disorientated. He said he could not find the path to his lodgings so had tried to cut across the fields. This resulted in him straying into the building site, where he was challenged by the security guard. Strong, angry words were exchanged, which led to a serious confrontation during which the lodger assaulted the guard. He hadn't meant to do it. He hadn't meant to kill anyone. But he had. Lives can change in a matter of seconds, and they can end even faster.

Within a quarter of an hour of being brought to the office, the lodger had admitted the assault. Shortly afterwards, he repeated it on tape. I can only say that I was very happy to have decided to have my Greggs bridies at that particular time and not to have charged the first suspect. This is how close it came to making a grave mistake but perhaps in the circumstances an understandable one.

The lodger appeared at the High Court in Glasgow, was found guilty and received a fairly hefty sentence. The first suspect, I believe, went back to being a security guard.

J.J.'S LAST CASE

As I got into the last of my 32 years in the police force, the pressure of work did not diminish. In fact, in my final year the total murder count in 'G' Division was on the increase and we had two separate killings in one weekend, real nasty ones at that – and that was on top of another murder inquiry which we already had in the Division. The new ones consisted of a shooting in Govan and another of a man who had been found dead in the street. Initially, it was thought that he had died from natural causes but a second post-mortem conducted by Marie Cassidy, now Chief State Pathologist for the Republic of Ireland, revealed that he had, in fact, died from a blow to the neck, possibly a karate-type blow. We were kept very busy but, as I have already said, I was extremely lucky with the team of officers I had working with me. We demanded high standards of one another and invariably these standards were delivered.

Three days before I was due to leave the job, we were alerted to another murder, this time in the Cardonald area. Normally, I would have stepped back and let DCI Harry Bell take control but he had been spirited away by headquarters to deal with an internal inquiry, so it was sleeves up and into it again.

An old man had been found dead in his flat in a high-rise block. A neighbour had noticed the door standing open as she went for the morning rolls. The old man had been slightly senile and, apparently, a bit of a nuisance – he often wandered around knocking on doors and causing mild havoc. The neighbour stuck her head around his open door shouting for the old man to see if he was OK. There was no answer, so she pushed her way in – with some difficulty, because something was blocking the door. She moved further in and saw that the house had been completely ransacked. Then she saw the man lying on the floor under a pile of clothing, which appeared to have been dragged from a wardrobe.

Arriving at the scene with the usual posse from the Identification

Bureau, who carefully photographed and dusted for fingerprints, we then removed the piles of clothing on top of the old fellow. We saw now that he had been battered about the head, bound and gagged. The post-mortem later revealed that the blows to the head, plus the fact that he had been gagged, had each contributed to his death. The house was in a total shambles and a tall fridge was jammed behind the front door, making access very difficult. I assumed that the perpetrator or perpetrators had used this to block the door while the flat was ransacked.

Within an hour of the corpse being found, I called in my full team of detectives and started a house-to-house inquiry to find out if any of the murdered man's neighbours had seen him the previous evening. I was still at the house consulting with the Procurator Fiscal and the casualty surgeon when one of my detective sergeants, Willie Erskine, told me that a young man on the next landing had seen the victim the night before wandering about on the stairs. Willie's nose was twitching about this guy, so he'd radioed in for a check to be made on him and, sure enough, there was a warrant out for him. The young man was about to go out with his girlfriend but another detective had been left with him while Willie spoke with me. I told him to take the guy back to the Office and lock him up on the warrant. If his girlfriend wanted to go out, she could tag along if she wished. Back at the Office, we could have a real chat with him. My nose was twitching, too.

Willie put him into an interview room and started to talk to him under tape-recorded conditions. The chap was obviously a junkie and a weak character, and it took only about an hour for him to admit that he had killed the old man in order to rob his flat. While he was being interviewed, his girlfriend was also being spoken to and she said that her boyfriend had brought a new tea set and some cutlery into the house the night before. She denied that she knew where these items had come from. The tea set and cutlery were retrieved from the young couple's house and identified as belonging to the murdered man.

When the young murderer was asked about the upright fridge jammed behind the front door, we expected his answer to be that this was to keep the door shut. However, he told us it had been his intention to actually steal the fridge but he could not get it out of the front door. The poor old man had been killed for an ancient tea set and some used cutlery.

This sad and needless death was my final murder arrest and the last case of my career. On the penultimate day of my service, I received a most unexpected call from headquarters. I was asked to have afternoon tea with Chief Constable Sir Leslie Sharp. I had met him before, during the inquiry into the death of Diane McInally, and found him to be a sensible man who knew what proper policing was about. Over tea and cakes, he started by asking me how many major murder inquiries I had been in charge of. Off the top of my head, I could not recall but on reflection realised it had been well over 150, and all properly investigated. He had done his homework on me, because he said, 'You have had a pretty colourful life.' I took it he was referring to the fact that I was in the middle of my second divorce, and I could not argue with him on this point. However, he then went on to congratulate me on my achievements as a police officer and my clearance rate regarding serious crime. I said, 'Well, I am sure, sir, none of my inquiries will come back to haunt the force in *Rough Justice*.' We had a very pleasant chat for over an hour regarding various cases.

I wish my last day on the job had been as pleasant. I was sitting in my room not believing that this day had finally come, when a uniformed chief inspector, the divisional staff officer, entered and asked for my Police Warrant Card. He said it was his duty to destroy it, as after this day it would not be valid. He received an angry growl in reply and a right earful as he beat a hasty retreat. I had carried that card proudly for 32 years and nobody else was going to take it and simply cut it up. So, my last action as a police officer was to personally tear up one of my most prized possessions, my own Police Warrant Card.

In over 30 years as a Glasgow cop, I'd come face-to-face with neds of all types. Smart ones, stupid ones, dangerous ones. I'd seen grown men weep as they came to terms with their crimes. I'd seen tough guys snarl defiance all the way through their arrest and trial. I'd been threatened by one of the city's most ruthless gangsters and I'd talked reasonably to perverted monsters in order to get them to confess. I'd laughed with fellow officers and grieved with them when the job turned lethal. I'd made that grim journey south in the blizzard with murder in my own heart.

When I walked away from Govan Police Office on that last day, I had more than a pension and the thanks of the Chief Constable. I had all these memories, good and bad.

And that, I suppose, is enough.